Economics

for Cambridge International AS & A Level

WORKBOOK

Colin Bamford

CAMBRIDGE
UNIVERSITY PRESS

University Printing House, Cambridge CB2 8BS, United Kingdom

One Liberty Plaza, 20th Floor, New York, NY 10006, USA

477 Williamstown Road, Port Melbourne, VIC 3207, Australia

314–321, 3rd Floor, Plot 3, Splendor Forum, Jasola District Centre, New Delhi – 110025, India

103 Penang Road, #05–06/07, Visioncrest Commercial, Singapore 238467

Cambridge University Press is part of the University of Cambridge.

It furthers the University's mission by disseminating knowledge in the pursuit of education, learning and research at the highest international levels of excellence.

www.cambridge.org
Information on this title: www.cambridge.org/9781108822794

© Cambridge University Press 2021

This publication is in copyright. Subject to statutory exception and to the provisions of relevant collective licensing agreements, no reproduction of any part may take place without the written permission of Cambridge University Press.

First published 2018
Second edition 2021

20 19 18 17 16 15 14 13 12 11 10 9 8 7 6 5

Printed in Malaysia by Vivar Printing

A catalogue record for this publication is available from the British Library

ISBN 978-1-108-82279-4 Paperback with Digital Access (2 Years)

Cambridge University Press has no responsibility for the persistence or accuracy of URLs for external or third-party internet websites referred to in this publication, and does not guarantee that any content on such websites is, or will remain, accurate or appropriate. Information regarding prices, travel timetables, and other factual information given in this work is correct at the time of first printing but Cambridge University Press does not guarantee the accuracy of such information thereafter.

....

NOTICE TO TEACHERS IN THE UK
It is illegal to reproduce any part of this work in material form (including photocopying and electronic storage) except under the following circumstances:
(i) where you are abiding by a licence granted to your school or institution by the Copyright Licensing Agency;
(ii) where no such licence exists, or where you wish to exceed the terms of a licence, and you have gained the written permission of Cambridge University Press;
(iii) where you are allowed to reproduce without permission under the provisions of Chapter 3 of the Copyright, Designs and Patents Act 1988, which covers, for example, the reproduction of short passages within certain types of educational anthology and reproduction for the purposes of setting examination questions.

....

Cambridge International copyright material in this publication is reproduced under licence and remains the intellectual property of Cambridge Assessment International Education.

Practice questions and sample answers have been written by the author. References to assessment and/or assessment preparation are the publisher's interpretation of the syllabus requirements and may not fully reflect the approach of Cambridge Assessment International Education.

Cambridge International recommends that teachers consider using a range of teaching and learning resources in preparing learners for assessment, based on their own professional judgement of their students' needs.

Third-party websites and resources referred to in this publication have not been endorsed by Cambridge Assessment International Education.

DEDICATED TEACHER AWARDS

Teachers play an important part in shaping futures. Our Dedicated Teacher Awards recognise the hard work that teachers put in every day.

Thank you to everyone who nominated this year. We have been inspired and moved by all of your stories. Well done to all of our nominees for your dedication to learning and for inspiring the next generation of thinkers, leaders and innovators.

Congratulations to our incredible winner and finalists!

WINNER
Patricia Abril
New Cambridge School, Colombia

Stanley Manaay
Salvacion National High School, Philippines

Tiffany Cavanagh
Trident College Solwezi, Zambia

Helen Comerford
Lumen Christi Catholic College, Australia

John Nicko Coyoca
University of San Jose-Recoletos, Philippines

Meera Rangarajan
RBK International Academy, India

For more information about our dedicated teachers and their stories, go to
dedicatedteacher.cambridge.org

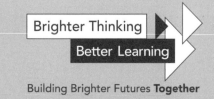

Building Brighter Futures **Together**

Contents

How to use this book	viii
Introduction	ix
Introduction to command words	x

1 Basic economic ideas and resource allocation (AS Level)   01
- 1 Scarcity, choice and opportunity cost   02
- 2 Economic methodology   05
- 3 Factors of production   08
- 4 Resource allocation in different economic systems   11
- 5 Production possibility curves   14
- 6 Classification of goods and services   17

2 The price system and the microeconomy (AS Level)   21
- 7 Demand and supply curves   22
- 8 Price elasticity, income elasticity and cross elasticity of demand   26
- 9 Price elasticity of supply   30
- 10 The interaction of demand and supply   33
- 11 Consumer and producer surplus   37

3 Government microeconomic intervention (AS Level)   41
- 12 Reasons for government intervention in markets   42
- 13 Methods and effects of government intervention in markets   45
- 14 Addressing income and wealth inequality   49

4 The macroeconomy (AS Level)   53
- 15 National income statistics   54
- 16 Introduction to the circular flow of income   58
- 17 Aggregate demand and aggregate supply analysis   61
- 18 Economic growth   65
- 19 Unemployment   69
- 20 Price stability   73

5 Government macroeconomic intervention (AS Level) — 77
- 21 Government macroeconomic policy objectives — 78
- 22 Fiscal policy — 81
- 23 Monetary policy — 85
- 24 Supply-side policy — 88

6 International economic issues (AS Level) — 91
- 25 The reasons for international trade — 92
- 26 Protectionism — 95
- 27 Current account of the balance of payments — 98
- 28 Exchange rates — 102
- 29 Policies to correct imbalances in the current account of the balance of payments — 105

7 The price system and the microeconomy (A Level) — 109
- 30 Utility — 110
- 31 Indifference curves and budget lines — 113
- 32 Efficiency and market failure — 117
- 33 Private costs and benefits, externalities and social costs and benefits — 121
- 34 Types of cost, revenue and profit, short-run and long-run production — 125
- 35 Different market structures — 129
- 36 Growth and survival of firms — 133
- 37 Differing objectives and policies of firms — 136

8 Government microeconomic intervention (A Level) — 141
- 38 Government policies to achieve efficient resource allocation and correct market failure — 142
- 39 Equity and redistribution of income and wealth — 146
- 40 Labour market forces and government intervention — 149

9 The macroeconomy (A Level) — 153
- 41 The circular flow of income — 154
- 42 Economic growth and sustainability — 158
- 43 Employment and unemployment — 161
- 44 Money and banking — 165

10 Government macroeconomic intervention (A Level) — **169**
- 45 Government macroeconomic policy objectives — 170
- 46 Links between macroeconomic problems and their interrelatedness — 173
- 47 Effectiveness of policy options to meet all macroeconomic objectives — 177

11 International economic issues (A Level) — **181**
- 48 Policies to correct disequilibrium in the balance of payments — 182
- 49 Exchange rates — 186
- 50 Economic development — 190
- 51 Characteristics of countries at different levels of development — 193
- 52 Relationship between countries at different levels of development — 197
- 53 Globalisation — 201

Acknowledgements — **204**

> How to use this book

Throughout this workbook, you will notice recurring features that are designed to help your learning. Here is a brief overview of what you will find.

LEARNING INTENTIONS

Learning intentions open each chapter. These help you with navigation through the workbook and indicate the important concepts in each topic. The learning intentions also map to the content in the *Cambridge International AS & A Level Economics Coursebook*.

Key skills exercises

These are scaffolded exercises which support your progression through the course and enable you to put into practice what you have learnt so far. The exercises have been clearly linked to the key skills that you need for economics.

- For knowledge and understanding exercises, there will be key content that you need to know and understand.
- For analysis exercises, you need to explain why or how something is important, or why or how it is an advantage or disadvantage.
- For evaluation exercises, you are required to make supported decisions, draw conclusions and give recommendations.

WORKED EXAMPLES

Worked examples provide you with sample answers (written by the author), in order to help you understand how to respond to questions using key skills. The answers are annotated with an abbreviated version of the relevant key skills:

- **[K]** Knowledge and understanding
- **[A]** Analysis
- **[E]** Evaluation.

KEY TERMS

These provide a reminder of the key definitions that you need to recall for each chapter topic.

TIPS

Tips are provided throughout this workbook to help with your learning. The tips provide you with additional practical guidance and advice to avoid confusion and to enhance your understanding of AS Level and A Level Economics.

PRACTICE QUESTIONS

These are more demanding questions that provide you with an opportunity to further practise what you have learnt in each topic.

Improve this answer

This offers you an opportunity to evaluate a sample answer to a question, which has been written by the author. Advice and guidance are provided in order to help you assess the answer. The relevant key skills are annotated as well.

Your challenge

After completing Improve this answer, you are then asked to apply the advice to your own answer.

You can find the answers to the exercises and practice questions in the digital workbook.

Note: Throughout the text, dollars ($) refer to US dollars, unless otherwise stated.

> Introduction

This workbook supports the Cambridge International AS & A Level Economics syllabus (9708) for examination from 2023. Its purpose is to support your learning as you progress through your course. By working through the many exercises, you will feel more confident about what you need to know to be a successful economics student.

The Workbook follows the syllabus in an exact way. Each chapter contains key skills exercises to remind you of the main subject content. The subject content is then applied to a present day economic issue or problem. Many of these features are drawn from countries where learners study this course. The questions are for each of the assessment objectives of the syllabus: knowledge and understanding, analysis and evaluation.

A second feature of each chapter is practice questions. These draw upon the content of the section and allow you to respond to multiple-choice, data response and essay questions. There is a mixture of these questions in each chapter. In addition, there is a sample written answer to one question. You are provided with feedback on the quality of this answer and then invited to see if you can improve it.

Answers to all key skills exercises, practice questions and improved answers are provided in the digital version of this resource (see the inside front cover for access information). Some answers are supplied in full. Others are in an outline form so that you can use the summary as the basis for writing your own answer.

As you progress through each chapter, you will realise that economics is not an exact science. Please bear this in mind when considering the online answers, especially those involving analysis and evaluation.

So, enjoy your study of economics. You will find this workbook to be an invaluable resource. I hope it will help you to succeed.

Colin Bamford

CAMBRIDGE INTERNATIONAL AS & A LEVEL ECONOMICS: WORKBOOK

Introduction to command words

The command words and definitions in this section are taken from the Cambridge International AS & A Level Economics syllabus (9708) for examination from 2023. You should always refer to the appropriate syllabus document for the year of your examination to confirm the details and for more information. The syllabus document is available on the Cambridge International website at www.cambridgeinternational.org.

The purpose of command words is to make it clear how you should approach answering a question. It is important that you understand what each command word is asking you to do.

These are the command words used in the Cambridge International AS & A Level Economics syllabus (9708) and in the practice questions in this workbook. In time and with practice, you will find that you can understand what skills you have to demonstrate in your answers to particular questions.

Command word	What it means	Guidance
Analyse	examine in detail to show meaning, identify elements and the relationship between them	You should write an answer that shows how the points in your answer link together, avoiding unnecessary detail.
Assess	make an informed judgement	You should write about both sides of a particular issue and then come to a supported conclusion about which, if any, is best.
Calculate	work out from given facts, figures or information	You should give a clear answer that includes the units involved (e.g. $).
Comment	give an informed opinion	You should give a view on a particular issue based on evidence and not unsupported opinion.
Compare	identify/comment on similarities and/or differences	You should make sure that your answer really does compare two things in terms of their similarities and differences and not just state what these things are.
Consider	review and respond to given information	You should make a brief point that contains some evaluation.
Define	give precise meaning	You should make sure that any definition is correct.
Demonstrate	show how or give an example	You should clearly show that your answer is drawn on evidence.
Describe	state the points of a topic / give characteristics and main features	You should give appropriate knowledge of a particular topic or issue.
Discuss	write about issue(s) or topic(s) in depth in a structured way	You should give a balanced account of both sides, for and against, an issue or argument.
Evaluate	judge or calculate the quality, importance, amount, or value of something	You should aim to make a reasoned judgement and include a supported conclusion on the merits or otherwise of something.
Explain	set out purposes or reasons / make the relationships between things evident / provide why and/or how and support with relevant evidence	You should write an answer that contains clearly identifiable reasons; you may have to draw upon data or other information to make your explanation clear.

Introduction to command words

Command word	What it means	Guidance
Give	produce an answer from a given source or recall/memory	You should provide an answer from memory or from a source that is familiar to you.
Identify	name/select/recognise	You should be precise about what you have identified.
Justify	support a case with evidence/argument	You should be confident that your justification is supported by relevant evidence.
Outline	set out main points	You should write a clear answer avoiding detail.
State	express in clear terms	You should give an uncomplicated yet valid factual statement.

> Unit 1

Basic economic ideas and resource allocation (AS Level)

> Chapter 1

Scarcity, choice and opportunity cost

LEARNING INTENTIONS

In this chapter you will:

- explain the fundamental economic problem of scarcity
- explain the need for individuals, firms and governments to make choices
- define the meaning of opportunity cost
- explain how opportunity cost results from the need to make choices
- explain the basic questions of resource allocation.

KEY TERMS

Choice   Fundamental economic problem   Needs   Opportunity cost   Resources   Scarcity   Wants

Key skills exercises

Knowledge and understanding

To answer the questions in this chapter, you need to know and understand:

- what the fundamental economic problem means
- why there is a need for individuals, firms and governments to make choices
- the meaning and significance of opportunity cost
- why opportunity cost is a consequence of the need to make choices
- the three basic questions of resource allocation.

1. What is the fundamental economic problem?
2. What are resources?
3. Describe the difference between a want and a need.
4. Why does scarcity occur?
5. Explain why individuals, firms and governments have to make choices.
6. Define the term 'opportunity cost'.
7. Describe the three basic questions of resource allocation.

> **TIP**
>
> Learners sometimes confuse what is meant by a need and what is meant by a want. A need is something that is essential. A want is something that someone would like to have.

1 Scarcity, choice and opportunity cost

Analysis

Government spending in India, 2014–2020

The Union budget of India for 2019–2020 included measures to improve the rural economy, strengthen agriculture and help those who are economically less privileged.

Figure 1.1 shows the pattern of estimated spending compared to average spending over the previous five budgets.

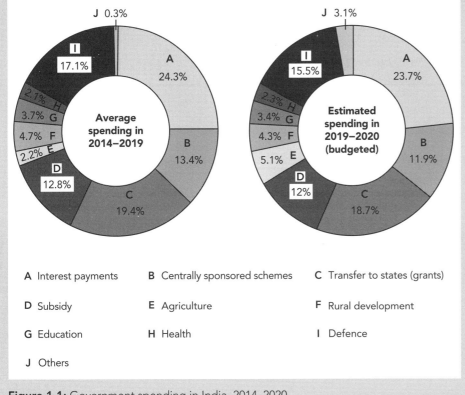

Figure 1.1: Government spending in India, 2014–2020

Source: Centre for Monitoring Indian Economy (CMIE)

The 2019–2020 budget is in deficit, with government spending more than government income.

8   Explain why the Indian government faces a fundamental economic problem when planning a budget.

9   What does the Indian government need to think about when setting its budget?

10 Explain how opportunity cost can be applied to the budgetary choices that have to be made.

11 Explain which of the three resource allocation questions the Indian government has addressed in its budget.

CAMBRIDGE INTERNATIONAL AS & A LEVEL ECONOMICS: WORKBOOK

PRACTICE QUESTIONS

Data response question

1. **a** Using the data in Figure 1.1, describe **three** ways in which the estimated 2019-2020 budget differs from average spending in 2014-2019.

   b Explain possible reasons for these three differences.

WORKED EXAMPLE FOR Q1

a Three differences are:
- expenditure on defence is planned to fall
- expenditure on agriculture is planned to increase
- expenditure on health is planned to increase **[K]**

b The new budget would appear to provide more government funding for the well-being of the people. This is a likely reason for the increase in healthcare funding. This will have an early and visible impact. The increased expenditure for agriculture is likely to improve the incomes of farmers and may be a way of increasing agricultural exports. Defence still takes up a large percentage of the budget compared to most other areas of government spending **[A]**.

Essay question

1. Explain how the fundamental economic problem affects your family **and** consider how opportunity cost can be applied to the problem of resource allocation.

Improve this answer

This is a sample answer to essay Q1.

> The fundamental economic problem is very important when studying economics. It affects firms, governments and families. All face the problem because resources are scarce and wants and needs are unlimited **[K]**. This means choices have to be made.
>
> In the case of my family, the income we receive is limited since there are only two family members who earn income from employment. Our wants and needs are many, so we have to make choices to make sure our limited income is shared in the best way possible **[A]**.
>
> All of us want more things. I would like a better mobile device or a newer scooter **[A]**. Until I start earning, these luxuries will have to wait.
>
> Opportunity cost is defined as the cost expressed in terms of the next best alternative that is sacrificed for something else **[A]**. Opportunity cost can apply to our family in all sorts of ways. Our limited income means that there is a fixed sum for groceries and other expenses but there is often other money left to spend. Ideally the different ways of spending this additional money should be ranked in order of their benefit for the family. This will allow informed choices to be made **[A]**.

Your challenge

See whether you can improve this answer. The answer covers the main parts of the question. The first paragraph is good but the remainder of the answer would benefit from being written in an analytical style. The answer should also define the difference between wants and needs. A better answer is given in the workbook answers – but write yours out first.

Chapter 2
Economic methodology

LEARNING INTENTIONS

In this chapter you will:

- explain why economics is a social science
- differentiate between facts and opinions (positive and normative statements)
- explain why economists use the term *ceteris paribus*
- explain when to refer to a time period such as 'short run', 'long run' and 'very long run'.

KEY TERMS

ceteris paribus   Long run   Macroeconomics   Microeconomics   Model   Normative statements
Positive statements   Short run   Very long run

Key skills exercises

Knowledge and understanding

To answer the questions in this chapter, you need to know and understand:

- the difference between microeconomics and macroeconomics
- why economists use models
- the difference between a positive statement and a normative statement
- the significance of the term *ceteris paribus*
- the difference between the short run, the long run and the very long run time periods.

1. What is microeconomics?
2. What is macroeconomics?
3. Explain why economists use models.
4. What is a positive statement?
5. What is a normative statement?
6. What is the significance of the term *ceteris paribus*?
7. Explain the difference between the short run, the long run and the very long run time periods.

Analysis

What is economics?

In your first economics lesson, you may have had very little idea what the subject was about. You were probably aware that economics has something to do with 'money' (but the subject is much wider) or even something to do with 'economical' (again the subject is wider).

The American Economic Association explains the social science of economics:

- Why are some countries rich and some countries poor?
- Why do women earn less than men?
- How can data help us understand the world?
- Why do we ignore information that could help us make better decisions?
- What causes recessions?

Economics can help us answer these questions.

Economics can be defined in a few different ways. It's the study of scarcity, the study of how people use resources and respond to incentives, or the study of decision-making. It often involves topics like wealth and finance, but it's not all about money. Economics is a broad discipline that helps us understand historical trends, interpret today's headlines, and make predictions about the coming years.

Economics ranges from the very small to the very large. The study of individual decisions is called microeconomics. The study of the economy as a whole is called macroeconomics. A microeconomist might focus on families' medical debt, whereas a macroeconomist might focus on sovereign debt*.

What do economists do?

Economists have all kinds of jobs, such as professors, government advisors, consultants, and private sector employees. Using theoretical models or empirical data, they evaluate programs, study human behavior, and explain social phenomena. And, their contributions inform everything from public policy to household decisions.

Economics intersects many disciplines. Its applications include health, gender, the environment, education, and immigration.

Why should I care about economics?

Economics affects everyone's lives. Learning about economic concepts can help you to understand the news, make financial decisions, shape public policy, and see the world in a new way.

* Sovereign debt: the amount of money a country's government has borrowed

Source: American Economic Association, *What is economics? Understanding the discipline*

Economists use both simple and complex models to represent real world situations. These models enhance our understanding of economic relationships and allow economists to make forecasts. Economic models often require just one variable to change – all other variables remain the same. This situation is called *ceteris paribus*.

2 Economic methodology

8 Which of the questions in the bulleted list on the previous page can be classified as microeconomics?

9 Which of the questions in the bulleted list on the previous page can be classified as macroeconomics?

10 Explain why all of the questions in the bulleted list on the previous page are normative statements.

11 Convert each of the questions in the bulleted list on the previous page into positive statements.

Evaluation

12 Comment on why economics is a social science.

PRACTICE QUESTION

Multiple-choice question

1 Which of these best describes the definition of the long run time period in economics?

   A No change can be made to production.

   B All resources used in production can be changed.

   C It is possible to think even further ahead in time.

   D Only one of the resources used in production can be changed.

WORKED EXAMPLE FOR Q1

B.

In the long run time period, all resources are variable. A is wrong and does not apply to any of the time periods used in economics. C could apply to any of the time periods. D refers to the short run [K].

This chapter does not contain an 'Improve this answer' feature.

Chapter 3
Factors of production

LEARNING INTENTIONS

In this chapter you will:

- define the meaning of factors of production: land, labour, capital and enterprise
- explain the importance of the factors of production
- describe the rewards to the factors of production
- explain the difference between human capital and physical capital
- explain the division of labour and specialisation
- explain the role of the entrepreneur in the organisation of factors of production in 21st century economies and as a risk taker.

KEY TERMS

Capital   Division of labour   Economic growth   Enterprise   Entrepreneur   Factors of production
High-income countries   Human capital   Labour   Land   Low-income countries   Lower middle-income countries
Physical capital   Specialisation

Key skills exercises

Knowledge and understanding

To answer the questions in this chapter, you need to know and understand:

- what is meant by a factor of production
- the meaning of land, labour, capital and enterprise as factors of production
- why factors of production are important
- how the use of factors of production is rewarded
- the difference between physical and human capital
- the role of the entrepreneur.

1. Define the term 'factor of production'.
2. Define 'land' as a factor of production.
3. Define 'labour' as a factor of production.
4. Define 'capital' as a factor of production.
5. Define 'enterprise' as a factor of production.
6. Describe the differences between a low-income country, a lower middle-income country, an upper middle-income country and a high-income country.
7. Explain the difference between physical capital and human capital.
8. Define the term 'economic growth'.
9. Explain the meaning of specialisation.
10. Explain the meaning of division of labour.

> **TIP**
>
> The classification of countries by the World Bank is used throughout the Workbook. It is based on Gross National Income (GNI) per head in 2018. The following levels apply:
> - Low-income country $1 025 or less
> - Lower middle-income country $1 026 to $3 995
> - Upper middle-income country $3 996 to $12 375
> - High-income country $12 376 and above
>
> You will find it helpful to familiarise yourself with which countries fall into which of the four categories. Note the wide range of GNI per head for middle-income countries.

Analysis

> **Mauritius: an upper middle-income economy**
>
> Mauritius, an island state in the Indian Ocean, has a population of 1.3m people. The country's economy is growing at a steady pace. Mauritius's economy is driven by construction and service industries such as tourism, banking and financial services and ICT. The country also has more traditional manufacturing and sugar production industries. However, the sugar production industry has declined in recent years.
>
> As a tourist destination, Mauritius is best known for its beaches, lagoons and reefs as well as inland forests and wildlife. The importance of tourism results in significant risks due to external shocks such as downturns in the economies of high-income countries and pressures to cut back on emissions from flying to combat climate change. Mauritius is also very vulnerable to tropical storms.
>
> The country's development has been financed internally and externally. Mauritius now has a growing number of wealthy entrepreneurs, such as Bashir Currimjee and P Arnaud Dalais, both of whom have headed companies with interests in all sectors of the island's economy. Although the unemployment rate is low, there is a lack of job opportunities for women. Youth unemployment is also an issue due to a skills mismatch and wages below the expectations of those entering the labour market.

11 Identify two examples of land in Mauritius.

12 Identify two examples of labour in Mauritius.

13 Identify two examples of capital in Mauritius.

14 Explain the risks facing entrepreneurs in Mauritius.

Evaluation

15 Consider how the two entrepreneurs have organised their businesses to minimise risk.

WORKED EXAMPLE FOR Q15

The second paragraph of the information states that Mauritius's economy is vulnerable to external shocks affecting the economies of high-income countries. The COVID-19 pandemic is an extreme example. Other external shocks include more regular recessions and a growing concern to reduce flying to combat climate change. Firms are also affected by annual tropical storms that hit the island [A]. The entrepreneurs have tried to minimise risk by diversifying their businesses to cover most of the key sectors that contribute to the island's economy. Tourism is the most vulnerable activity. Banking, finance and ICT are likely to be more stable [E].

CAMBRIDGE INTERNATIONAL AS & A LEVEL ECONOMICS: WORKBOOK

PRACTICE QUESTIONS

Multiple-choice question

1 Human capital is often referred to as a form of investment. Why is this?

   A Labour is required to produce all goods and services.

   B Improved human capital can lead to increased economic growth.

   C Human capital is costly like any investment.

   D Top earners are able to invest some of their earnings.

Essay questions

1 Explain how capital and labour are needed for the manufacture of cotton garments **and** consider how an entrepreneur responds to an increase in demand for these garments.

2 Explain the difference between human capital and physical capital **and** consider which is likely to be most important for an entrepreneur to have when growing a business.

> **TIP**
>
> When writing essays avoid the use of 'I'. Try to make your answers impersonal.

Improve this answer

This is a sample answer to essay Q1.

A factor of production is something that is required in an economy for production to take place. Economists recognise four, namely land, labour, capital and enterprise **[K]**. I will now explain what is meant by capital and labour and then how each are needed in the manufacture of cotton garments.

Capital is defined as an aid to production that is human-made. It refers to many different things such as factory buildings, machinery, power supplies, IT systems, warehouses and container vessels. In a garment manufacturing business, the factory building and the machinery used to manufacture garments are examples of capital **[K]**. In a competitive industry, such as clothing, the quality of the capital employed rather than quantity is of considerable relevance. Old machinery that keeps breaking down is more likely to restrict production and productivity than the latest production technology, even if this is no more than high-quality sewing machines **[A]**.

The quality and quantity of labour is also important. A garment manufacturer is likely to need most staff to have particular skills that can be applied in the production process. If there is a skill shortage then workers will have to be trained. Most manufacturers will also need low skilled and high skilled workers to complete the input of labour into the production process **[A]**.

Enterprise is the role of the owner of the garment factory. This person needs to be able to know what is required in order to produce and sell the garments that are produced **[A]**. If successful, the business will grow.

Your challenge

See whether you can improve this answer. The first three paragraphs are generally good. Now, look at the concluding (final) paragraph. The paragraph is weak and does not explain how an entrepreneur might respond to an increase in demand for garments. Your challenge is write a new concluding paragraph. A better answer is given in the workbook answers – but write yours out first.

Chapter 4
Resource allocation in different economic systems

LEARNING INTENTIONS

In this chapter you will:

- explain decision-making in market, planned and mixed economic systems
- analyse the advantages and disadvantages of resource allocation in market, planned and mixed economic systems.

KEY TERMS

Asian Tiger economy   Economic system   Emerging economy   Market economy   Market mechanism
Mixed economy   Planned economy   Private sector   Privatisation   Productive resources   Public sector

Key skills exercises

Knowledge and understanding

To answer the questions in this chapter, you need to know and understand:

- why choices have to be made in any economic system
- the role of the market mechanism in market, planned and mixed economies
- the role of government in market, planned and mixed economies
- the role of the private sector and the public sector in market, planned and mixed economies.

1 Define the term 'market system'.
2 Define the term 'market economy'. Give an example of a market economy.
3 Define the term 'planned economy'. Give an example of a planned economy.
4 Define the term 'mixed economy'. Give an example of a mixed economy.
5 Compare the roles of the market and government in:
   a market economies
   b planned economies
   c mixed economies.
6 Compare the roles of the private sector and the public sector in a mixed economy.
7 Describe the term 'emerging economy'. Give an example of an emerging economy.

Analysis

Poland's transformation to a mixed economy

Poland is one of the fastest growing economies in the world. The country's transformation from a planned economy to a more market-orientated economy began in 1989 with the end of communism.

Before 1989, Poland experienced the problems of most planned economies. Shops lacked supplies of meat, as well as everyday items such as soap and razor blades. Queuing was an accepted part of daily life. In cities like Krakow, the air was badly polluted from coal-burning steelworks and from the exhausts of poorly made Russian and East German vehicles.

Since 1989, Poland's GDP has increased by over 300%. Government expenditure as a percentage of GDP was estimated to be 41% in 2018, a drop of 10% since 2008. This figure is now very similar to that of the UK. The transformation has come about through foreign investment, Polish entrepreneurs prepared to take risks and the motivation of hard-working people keen to improve their standard of living. Poland's economic growth is also linked to the millions of euros in funding from the European Union (EU).

The costs of transition to a more market economy need to be considered. Millions of jobs have been lost from state-owned farms, food manufacturing and from heavy industries such as coal, steel and cement production. Hundreds of thousands of Polish people have migrated to other EU countries in search of a better life.

Many former migrants have now returned to Poland. The economy is relatively stable, new jobs are being created and manufacturing productivity has increased. It is a measure of success that car ownership in Poland is at about the same level as in France and Germany.

8 Explain some of the resource allocation problems that Poland had with its planned economy.

9 Explain how it is possible to tell if an economy like Poland is being transformed from a planned economy to one where market forces have an increasing role in decision-making.

10 Explain why Poland is now a mixed economy.

11 Analyse how free market forces have helped to increase Poland's rate of economic growth.

Evaluation

12 Consider the costs and benefits of Poland's transformation to a market economy.

WORKED EXAMPLE FOR Q12

The information refers to various costs and benefits. One of the first and most serious costs is that of increased unemployment [K]. In planned economies, jobs were virtually guaranteed, particularly in inefficient state-owned factories making iron and steel, vehicles and in coal mining. Many workers migrated once Poland became a full member of the EU. This can be considered a cost to the Polish economy, especially if the migrants were professional workers [A]. The benefits have come through increased economic growth [K]. In particular, there has been inward investment from elsewhere in the EU, creating new jobs. Polish agriculture has also benefited from access to new EU markets and through subsidised farm prices [A].

TIP

Learners often forget that it can take many years for an economy to move from a planned economy to one like Poland that has more of the features of a market economy. This is because it takes time for state-owned businesses to be sold off and for private sector buyers to accumulate the finance and expertise to run many new enterprises. In the cases of Poland, Hungary and the Baltic states of Estonia, Latvia and Lithuania, this process has taken over 20 years.

4 Resource allocation in different economic systems

PRACTICE QUESTIONS

Multiple-choice question

1 Which of these is a characteristic only of a pure market economy?

   A   Prices are mainly determined by supply and demand.

   B   International trade is not encouraged.

   C   The government should regulate competition in markets.

   D   The public sector should only provide public goods.

Essay questions

1 Compare the ways in which resources are allocated in a market economy and in a mixed economy **and** consider in which type of economy consumers' needs are best provided for.

2 Explain how an economy moves from a planned to a mixed economy **and** consider whether this can only succeed with enterprise.

Improve this answer

This is a sample answer to essay Q2.

> A planned economy is one that has a strong central government function. The government owns all industries and plans the allocation of resources **[K]**. The private sector has little involvement apart from owning small shops and restaurants. There is therefore no particular place for enterprise. Today, North Korea and to a lesser extent Vietnam are planned economies **[K]**.
>
> A mixed economy has both a market and a government sector. Both allocate resources for the benefit of their populations. The government provides public goods and some merit goods, especially for those who are in need. There may be a little state ownership but most productive resources are owned by the private sector following privatisation. In mixed economies there are opportunities for enterprising business people to succeed **[A]**.

Your challenge

See whether you can improve this answer. It contains some basic knowledge that is relevant to the question. The answer is short and lacks detail. It would benefit from a description of the process of moving from a planned to a mixed economy. A few examples of economies to which the process can be applied would also add to the answer's relevance. The second part of the question is only dealt with very briefly at the end. The consideration of the importance of enterprise needs to be expanded for the answer to demonstrate evaluation skills. A better answer is given in the workbook answers – but write yours out first.

Chapter 5
Production possibility curves

> **LEARNING INTENTIONS**
>
> In this chapter you will:
>
> - explain the meaning and purpose of a production possibility curve
> - explain the shape of the production possibility curve, including the difference between constant opportunity costs and increasing opportunity costs
> - analyse the causes and consequences of shifts in a production possibility curve
> - discuss the significance of a position within a production possibility curve.

> **KEY TERMS**
>
> Productive capacity   Production possibility curve (PPC)   Trade-off

Key skills exercises

Knowledge and understanding

To answer the questions in this chapter, you need to know and understand:

- the features of a PPC
- why a PPC is sometimes referred to as a production possibility frontier
- the significance of any point located on the PPC
- the causes and consequences of a shift in the PPC
- how opportunity cost can be applied to explain the shape of a PPC.

1. Outline the characteristics of a PPC.
2. Why is a PPC also known as a production possibility frontier?
3. What is shown by a point on a PPC?
4. What is indicated by a movement along a PPC?
5. Why might an economy operate from a point within its PPC?
6. Explain why a point outside the PPC is not a possible outcome.

5 Production possibility curves

Analysis

Difficult choices facing a lower middle-income country

The production possibility curve in Figure 5.1 shows the choices that are facing a lower middle-income country that is seeking to increase its rate of economic growth through developing a bigger manufacturing sector.

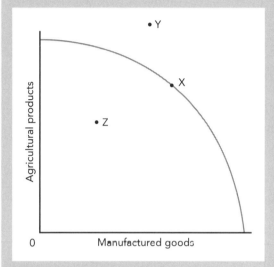

Figure 5.1: Production possibility curve

> **TIP**
>
> Learners sometimes wrongly label the axes of a PPC diagram. A common error is to label them 'Price' and 'Quantity'. You can use labels like those in Figure 5.1, or you could use 'Good A' and 'Good B' or any two other named goods.

7 Explain what the PPC in Figure 5.1 shows.

8 Explain the difference between points Y and Z in Figure 5.1.

9 Analyse the trade-off if the economy moves along the PPC from point X.

10 Analyse how an increase in productive capacity in manufacturing affects the shape of the PPC.

WORKED EXAMPLE FOR Q10

An increase in the productive capacity (productivity) in manufacturing is shown by a 'pivot' of the PPC from its maximum point on the vertical axis. This means that more manufactured goods can be produced with no change in resources **[A]**. The production of agricultural goods is unchanged.

11 Analyse how economic growth affects the position of the PPC.

12 Analyse how a change in employment affects point Z within the PPC.

13 Analyse how opportunity cost can be applied to explain the shape of the PPC.

Evaluation

14 Consider the strengths and weaknesses of the country's policy to expand its manufacturing sector.

15 Consider the value and the limitations of the PPC model.

CAMBRIDGE INTERNATIONAL AS & A LEVEL ECONOMICS: WORKBOOK

PRACTICE QUESTIONS

Multiple-choice question

1   Figure 5.1 shows a production possibility curve (PPC).

    What would be most likely to cause an outward shift of the PPC?

    A   An increase in the General Sales Tax on manufactured goods.

    B   Improvements to the quality of seeds available to farmers.

    C   More agricultural land being used for housing.

    D   An increase in the secondary school leaving age.

Essay questions

1   With the help of a production possibility diagram, explain how governments face increasing opportunity cost when deciding how to allocate resources **and** consider if the opportunity cost involved is ever zero.

2   Discuss whether enterprise is the most important economic reason why the production possibility curve of a country shifts outwards.

Improve this answer

This is a sample answer to essay Q2.

> A production possibility curve (PPC) shows the maximum level of output that a country can achieve, given its current resources and state of technology **[K]**. These assumptions are important when considering how the PPC of an economy might shift from its current position.
>
> Factors of production include land, labour, capital and enterprise. They are the main reasons why the PPC shifts outwards, resulting in an increase in the maximum level of output of both products. The shift can come about due to significantly more labour being employed, firms investing more resources in capital equipment or especially for agriculture, a significant increase in the land available for cultivation to produce marketable produce **[A]**.
>
> In some respects, enterprise is responsible for making the shift of the PPC happen. Through an entrepreneur, the factors of production can be organised and put together in such a way to cause a shift outwards of the PPC **[A]**. This therefore makes enterprise the most important factor in making the shift happen.

Your challenge

See whether you can improve this answer. The answer needs to be more detailed. The first two paragraphs cover some basic ideas. The final paragraph is too brief – it fails to address the key point of the question (the role of enterprise in shifting the PPC outwards). There is little attempt to evaluate. Your challenge is to write two additional paragraphs. A better answer is given in the workbook answers – but write yours out first.

Chapter 6
Classification of goods and services

LEARNING INTENTIONS

In this chapter you will:

- explain the meaning and importance of free goods and private goods (economic goods)
- explain the meaning and importance of public goods
- explain the meaning and importance of merit goods and demerit goods
- analyse how underconsumption of merit goods results from imperfect information in the market
- analyse how overconsumption of demerit goods results from imperfect information in the market.

KEY TERMS

Demerit good   Disposable income   Excludability   Free goods   Free rider   Information failure   Merit good
Non-excludable   Non-rival   Private goods   Public goods   Pure public good   Quasi-public good   Rivalry

Key skills exercises

Knowledge and understanding

To answer the questions in this chapter, you need to know and understand:

- the difference between free goods and private goods
- the characteristics of public goods
- the reasons why public goods are provided by governments
- the characteristics of merit goods
- the reasons why merit goods are provided by a government and the private sector
- the characteristics of demerit goods
- the reasons why governments seek to regulate use of demerit goods.

1. Describe the characteristics of a free good.
2. Describe the characteristics of a private good.
3. Describe 'non-excludable' in the context of a public good.
4. Describe 'non-rival' in the context of a public good.
5. Give the characteristics of a quasi-public good.
6. Explain what is meant by a 'free rider' in the context of a public good.
7. Explain **two** examples of a public good.
8. Describe 'information failure'.
9. Explain how information failure applies to a merit good.

TIP

Learners often confuse non-excludable and non-rival. To avoid this confusion, think of the difference by way of an example such as a local fire service. Everybody can use it (non-excludable) and all will get the same benefit from using it (non-rival).

10 Explain **two** examples of a merit good.

11 Explain how information failure applies to a 'demerit good'.

12 Explain **two** examples of a demerit good.

Analysis

Healthcare expenditure in Africa

Figure 6.1 shows the average expenditure per head on healthcare in Africa in terms of US dollars and as a percentage of GDP. Both measures are low when compared to more developed economies.

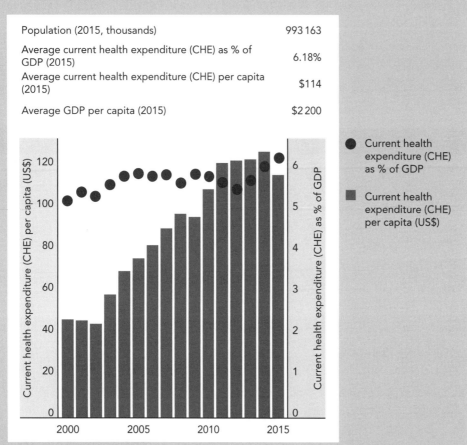

Figure 6.1: Current health expenditures per capita and as share of GDP, Africa 2000–2015 (in $)

Source: African Regional Health Expenditure Dashboard, WHO

Healthcare is classified by economists as a merit good. In some countries, for example in the UK, healthcare is largely provided free of charge at the point of consumption and is funded from taxation. Governments face the fundamental economic problem of there not being sufficient resources to fund all that is needed and have to increasingly rely on the private sector to provide healthcare services.

The same is true for most African countries, where cash-strapped governments are struggling to meet a huge shortfall in funding. To close the gap, they must look to private capital to relieve the pressure on over-stretched government-run facilities.

13 Explain how healthcare expenditure in Africa has changed since 2000.

> **WORKED EXAMPLE FOR Q13**
>
> Both measures of healthcare spending have an upward trend since 2000 [K]. Expenditure as a percentage of GDP fluctuates more than expenditure per head [K]. Expenditure as a percentage of GDP tends to be adversely affected by economic downturns such as in 2008. Health expenditure per head has increased by at least 250% from 2000 to 2015 [A].

14 How does information failure apply in the provision of healthcare?

15 Explain whether the provision of healthcare services by the private sector is a private good.

16 Apply opportunity cost to the need for African governments to increase their expenditure on healthcare.

Evaluation

17 Comment on whether healthcare in Africa should be free to all.

18 Discuss the benefits and costs to individuals and the African economy of having a healthier population.

PRACTICE QUESTIONS

Multiple-choice question

1 Which of these is an appropriate reason for a government in a middle-income country to fund university tuition fees?

  A Less government funding can be allocated to defence.

  B More graduates will go abroad to work.

  C There are longer-term benefits for the economy such as an increased economic growth rate.

  D There will be a negative impact on the distribution of income.

Essay questions

1 Explain why demerit goods are only provided by the private sector **and** consider whether the private sector alone should provide merit goods.

2 Explain the characteristics of pure public goods **and** consider why some goods are classified as quasi-public goods.

3 Explain why higher education is a merit good **and** consider whether in a free market the price charged reflects the true value to higher education students.

> **TIP**
>
> Why not build up a list of different types of good from countries that are known to you? This will help you to understand the different types of good.

CONTINUED

Improve this answer

This is a sample answer to essay Q2.

> A public good is something that is provided by the government for the benefit of the people. It has to be paid for out of taxation. An example is the army in my country. Other examples are street lights and public libraries **[K]**.
>
> There are two characteristics as to why the above examples are public goods. These are called non-rival and non-excludable **[K]**. Let me now explain what each means.
>
> Non-rival means everyone benefits. Nobody can be excluded from benefiting from the army or street lights. Everybody can benefit in the same way. Non-excludable means that even if you have not paid any taxes towards paying for the public good, you are still able to benefit from it **[A]**. Such people are called free-riders.
>
> A quasi-public good is not the same as a pure public good. This type of public good is one where neither of the characteristics is fully applied **[K]**. An example is a pay road. You cannot use the road if you have not paid the charge. It is non-rival as once you have paid to use a road, you have the same use of it as other drivers **[A]**.

Your challenge

See whether you can improve this answer. The answer is weak in terms of its knowledge of public goods and its application. It is confused over the meaning of non-rival. The answer implies that it is the same as non-excludable. Street lights are acceptable as a public good, but a public library is a merit good as some people can be excluded. A better answer is given in the workbook answers – but write yours out first.

> Unit 2
The price system and the microeconomy (AS Level)

Chapter 7
Demand and supply curves

LEARNING INTENTIONS

In this chapter you will:
- define the meaning of effective demand
- explain the importance of individual and market demand and supply
- explain the factors that affect demand
- explain the factors that affect supply
- analyse the causes of a shift in the demand curve (D)
- analyse the causes of a shift in the supply curve (S)
- distinguish between a shift in the demand or supply curve and the movement along these curves.

KEY TERMS

Complement   Consumers   Contraction of demand or supply   Demand   Demand curve   Demand schedule
Effective demand   Extension of demand or supply   Indirect tax   Inferior goods   Joint demand   Market
Market demand   Movement up and down (along) a demand curve   Normal goods   Notional demand
Price mechanism   Subsidy   Substitute   Supply   Supply chain   Supply curve   Supply schedule

Key skills exercises

Knowledge and understanding

To answer the questions in this chapter, you need to know and understand:
- how the price mechanism works in a market
- individual and market demand curves
- individual and market supply curves
- the reason for a movement up and down (along) a demand curve
- the factors that affect the demand for goods and services
- the reason for a movement up and down a supply curve
- the factors that affect the supply of goods and services
- the causes of a shift in a demand curve
- the causes of a shift in a supply curve.

1 Define the 'price mechanism'.
2 Define a 'market'.
3 State what is meant by 'demand'.
4 State what is meant by 'supply'.
5 Explain the difference between notional demand and effective demand.
6 Describe what is shown by a demand curve.

7   Describe what is shown by a supply curve.

8   What is the difference between normal goods and inferior goods?

9   What causes movement along a demand curve?

10   What causes movement along a supply curve?

11   Explain the factors that affect the demand for goods and services.

12   Explain the factors that affect the supply of goods and services.

Analysis

US consumers losing taste for orange juice

The orange juice industry around the world had a difficult year in 2017. The industry faced demand and supply conditions on a scale not experienced for more than ten years.

The demand for orange juice has been falling, particularly in its two main markets, the USA and Europe (see Figure 7.1 for the USA). This has been for various reasons, such as increasing concerns about sugar and its links to obesity and diabetes through the excessive consumption of orange juice. Other factors have been the growing consumption of apple juice and smoothies. Lifestyle factors are also relevant, especially in the USA where fewer people now eat a sit-down breakfast.

The supply issues are complex. In 2017, disease affected the oranges harvest in Mexico; drought hit production in California and Brazil. To add to the problems, a hurricane devastated orchards in Florida and Cuba. In contrast, elsewhere in Spain and Morocco, record harvests were reported.

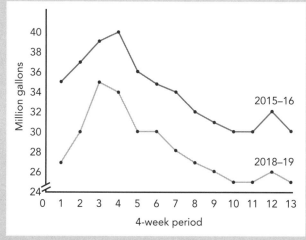

Figure 7.1: Retail orange juice sales in millions of gallons in the USA, 2015–16 and 2018–19

Source: IEG Vu Agribusiness Intelligence

13   Analyse why the supply of orange juice is unstable and how this affects the global price of orange juice.

14   Analyse how a reduction in the price of orange juice is likely to affect the quantity demanded.

15   Analyse how increasing awareness of obesity is likely to affect the demand for orange juice in the USA.

> **TIP**
>
> Learners often confuse a movement along a demand or supply curve and a shift to the right or left of these curves. Remember that a movement up or down a demand or supply curve is due to a change in price *alone*. A shift is a consequence of a change in any of the factors that determine demand or supply.

Evaluation

16 Comment on what is likely to be the most important reason for the declining sales of orange juice in the USA.

17 Discuss whether demand-side or supply-side factors are more important in determining the global price of orange juice.

PRACTICE QUESTIONS

Data response question

1   a Using the data in Figure 7.1, compare the US sales of orange juice between 2015-16 and 2018-19.
    b Explain **two** reasons for the changes you have identified.

WORKED EXAMPLE FOR Q1

a The sales of orange juice in 2018-19 are consistently lower than sales in 2015-16 **[K]**.

The monthly pattern of sales in both years is similar except for period 5 in 2018-19 **[K]**.

b Increasing concerns about sugar consumption **[K]**. These concerns have reduced the demand for orange juice as there have been concerns that drinking too much of the juice can lead to the onset of diabetes and obesity **[A]**.

Growing consumption of apple juice and smoothies **[K]**. These products are substitutes for orange juice. An increase in their demand has led to a fall in consumption of orange juice **[A]**.

Essay questions

1 Explain the factors that are likely to determine the demand for holidays by international tourists to an exotic island such as Mauritius **and** consider which of these factors is likely to be most important.

2 A producer of avocados is experiencing an increase in demand which cannot be met from existing supply. With the help of demand and supply curve diagrams, explain whether the producer should increase the price of avocados or consider planting more trees to increase production.

Improve this answer

This is a sample answer to essay Q1.

> According to economic theory, there are various factors that determine the demand for a product. I will now list these and then take each one in turn to explain their relevance in determining the demand for holidays by international tourists to Mauritius. The factors are
> - income
> - price and availability of substitutes and complements
> - fashion, taste, attitudes **[K]**.
>
> Mauritius is an exotic destination in the Indian Ocean. I believe from what I have read that it mainly attracts tourists from the better off countries in Europe. This would seem to indicate that income, or more correctly disposable income is an important reason when international tourists are considering a holiday in Mauritius **[A]**. It would seem to be a superior good **[A]**.
>
> International tourism is a competitive business and tourists will also be considering other destinations as well as Mauritius. So the price of substitutes is relevant, particularly those substitutes that offer very similar facilities

CONTINUED

to Mauritius. The price of complements such as hotel accommodation, the cost of food, drink and other activities, may also have a bearing on whether tourists choose to holiday in Mauritius **[A]**.

Finally, there are a range of other factors, it could be that Mauritius does not appeal to some groups (for example, older people) or that they have been influenced about what they have read or seen on TV about Mauritius **[A]**. These factors are impossible to quantify but could be of significance when the final decision is taken **[E]**.

Of these factors, I feel that the last ones (fashion, taste and attitudes) are going to be the most important reasons why international tourists want to take a holiday in Mauritius.

Your challenge

See whether you can improve this answer. The answer has some good points. It is well structured and covers the three main factors that determine the demand for a product. The paragraph that begins 'Finally, there are a range of other factors…' is particularly good and contains some evaluation. The last paragraph is weak – it needs to explain more fully why the other two factors are not as important. A better answer is given in the workbook answers – but write yours out first.

> Chapter 8
Price elasticity, income elasticity and cross elasticity of demand

LEARNING INTENTIONS

In this chapter you will:

- define the meaning of price elasticity, income elasticity and cross elasticity of demand (PED, YED, XED)
- use formulae to calculate price elasticity, income elasticity and cross elasticity of demand
- explain the importance of relative percentage changes, the size and sign of the coefficient in relation to price elasticity, income elasticity and cross elasticity of demand
- describe elasticity values: perfectly elastic, (highly) elastic, unitary elasticity, (highly) inelastic, perfectly inelastic
- explain the variation in price elasticity of demand along the length of a straight-line demand curve
- analyse the factors that affect price, income and cross elasticity of demand
- analyse the relationship between price elasticity of demand and total expenditure on a product
- discuss how estimates of price, income and cross elasticity of demand can affect decision-making.

KEY TERMS

Cross elasticity of demand (XED)   Elastic   Elasticity   Income elasticity of demand (YED)   Inelastic
Inferior good   Necessity good   Normal good   Perfectly elastic   Perfectly inelastic   Price elastic
Price elasticity of demand (PED)   Price inelastic   Superior good   Unit elasticity

Key skills exercises

Knowledge and understanding

To answer the questions in this chapter, you need to know and understand:

- the difference between 'elastic' and 'inelastic'.
- the meaning of price elasticity of demand, income elasticity of demand and cross elasticity of demand
- the formulae and how to calculate estimates of price elasticity of demand, income elasticity of demand and cross elasticity of demand
- the factors affecting price elasticity of demand, income elasticity of demand and cross elasticity of demand
- the difference between normal goods, inferior goods, necessity goods and superior goods

8 Price elasticity, income elasticity and cross elasticity of demand

- the difference between substitutes and complements
- the ways in which a business can make use of estimates of price elasticity of demand, income elasticity of demand and cross elasticity of demand.

1. Compare the terms 'elastic' and 'inelastic'.
2. Define price elasticity of demand and give its formula.
3. What is the difference between price elastic and price inelastic?
4. Explain the **three** factors that affect the price elasticity of demand for a good or service.
5. Define income elasticity of demand and give its formula.
6. What is the difference between income elastic and income inelastic?
7. Explain how goods are classified in relation to changes in the income of consumers.
8. Define cross elasticity of demand and give its formula.
9. How does cross elasticity of demand differentiate between a substitute and a complement?

> **TIP**
>
> Learners often use the wrong formula for calculating cross elasticities of demand. It is useful to remember that this measure looks at changes in the price and quantity of *two different* goods. The formulae for price elasticity of demand and income elasticity of demand use changes in quantity of *one* good.

Analysis

Good advice for Mr Patel?

Mr Patel owns a small restaurant in Lahore, Pakistan. He is increasingly concerned that sales of food have been falling since he increased prices a few months ago. His son, an economics student, has recently collected data relating to his father's restaurant as part of a class activity. He has found out the following information.

	Previous quantity/price (in Pakistani rupees)	Current quantity/price (in Pakistani rupees)
Quantity of meals demanded per week	500	425
Price of meals	200	220

Table 8.1: Data for Mr Patel's restaurant

Mr Patel's son has also estimated that the income elasticity of demand for meals at his father's restaurant is –0.8 and that the cross elasticity of demand in relation to a change in price of meals at a neighbouring restaurant is +1.2.

10. Calculate the price elasticity of demand for meals at Mr Patel's restaurant and explain what the estimate means.
11. Explain what Mr Patel's son's estimate of income elasticity of demand means.
12. Explain what Mr Patel's son's estimate of cross elasticity of demand means.

Evaluation

13. Comment on the reliability of the elasticity estimates made by Mr Patel's son.
14. Discuss what use Mr Patel might make of the three elasticity estimates and say which would be of most use to his restaurant business in the long run.

> **TIP**
>
> Note how the wording of Questions 10–14 consistently refers to the elasticity calculations as 'estimates'. This is because of the difficulty of collecting data from two different time periods. Learners sometimes miss this important point.

CAMBRIDGE INTERNATIONAL AS & A LEVEL ECONOMICS: WORKBOOK

WORKED EXAMPLE FOR Q14

The estimate of 1.5 for price elasticity of demand indicates that the quantity of meals demanded at Mr Patel's restaurant is price elastic. This means demand is price sensitive. Mr Patel's meals also appear to be an inferior good as the income elasticity of demand is negative. The cross elasticity of demand estimate indicates there are substitute meals available at a neighbouring restaurant **[A]**. None of this is particularly good news for Mr Patel **[E]**.

One possibility might be to reduce the price of meals. A 10% reduction in price would lead to a 15% increase in the number of meals taken. This would increase revenue and be likely to attract some customers from the competitor **[A]**. This could be risky as it would reinforce the perception of Mr Patel's meals being a type of inferior good **[E]**.

The income elasticity of demand estimate will be of most use in the long run. It indicates that Mr Patel should take a critical look at his product to make it a normal good that is price inelastic in demand. This should set it apart from his competitor's meals **[E]**.

PRACTICE QUESTIONS

Multiple-choice question

1 The monthly income of a worker increases from $1000 to $1200. As a result their demand for pizzas increases from 5 to 7 each month.

Which is the correct calculation and interpretation of income elasticity of demand?

A	0.2	income elastic
B	0.2	income inelastic
C	2.0	income elastic
D	2.0	income inelastic

Essay questions

1 Explain the factors that can affect the price elasticity of demand for a product **and** consider which of these is most important.
2 Explain how income elasticity of demand can be used to distinguish between normal, inferior and superior goods **and** consider any problems of applying this classification.
3 Discuss whether knowledge of income elasticity of demand is likely to be more useful than knowledge of cross elasticities of demand to a government agency that is seeking to grow its market for international tourists.

Improve this answer

This is a sample answer to essay Q3.

> Income elasticity is calculated by looking at the way in which the quantity that is demanded responds to a change in income **[K]**. In this case, if the YED is positive, the tourist place can expect more tourists when the income level rises **[A]**. Cross elasticity is different and is used to show how the demand for one product is affected by a change in price of another **[K]**.
>
> Many resorts in Asia attract international visitors. The change in income referred to is a change in the tourist's own country, as this affects their disposable income to spend on holidays. When this increases, they will really like to go to places like Bali, Goa and Phuket, all of which represent a new experience compared to where they live. Knowing this information will help the government agency **[A]**.

8 Price elasticity, income elasticity and cross elasticity of demand

CONTINUED

Cross elasticity helps also. This is because it can be used to throw light on which destinations compete with each other. For example, the places mentioned and Caribbean islands tend to have similar facilities for tourists. Government agencies will again find this information useful as it helps them know who they are competing with [A]. If they know all of this they can plan to grow their numbers.

Your challenge

See whether you can improve this answer. The answer is well structured, but it is descriptive rather than analytical. The answer lacks precision, in particular in the way the two elasticity concepts are defined and explained. There needs to be more application of income elasticity of demand and cross elasticity of demand to the context of a country seeking to develop international tourism. The evaluation is not adequate. Ideally the evaluation should be a clear assessment of which of the two elasticity measures is going to be most useful to the government. A better answer is written in the workbook answers – but write yours out first.

> Chapter 9
Price elasticity of supply

LEARNING INTENTIONS

In this chapter you will:

- define the meaning of price elasticity of supply (PES)
- calculate price elasticity of supply using the formula
- explain the significance of the relative percentage changes, the size and sign of the coefficient of price elasticity of supply
- analyse the factors affecting price elasticity of supply
- discuss how price elasticity of supply is related to the speed and ease with which producers react to changed market conditions.

KEY TERMS

Price elastic supply   Price elasticity of supply (PES)   Price inelastic supply

Key skills exercises

Knowledge and understanding

To answer the questions in this chapter, you need to know and understand:

- the meaning of price elasticity of supply
- the difference between 'price elastic' and 'price inelastic' supply
- how to calculate price elasticity of supply using the formula
- the factors affecting price elasticity of supply
- the ways in which producers can make use of estimates of price elasticity of supply.

1 Define price elasticity of supply and give the formula of price elasticity of supply.
2 What is the difference between 'price elastic' and 'price inelastic' supply?
3 Explain **three** factors that affect the price elasticity of supply for a good or service.

Analysis

The supply of solar-powered water pumps in Kenya

A producer of solar-powered water pumps in Kenya believes that the firm can respond quickly to price changes in the market.

At a price of $1000 each, the producer is willing to supply 200 units. When price suddenly increases to $1250, the producer supplies 220 units.

The Kenyan producer's main competitor is a large German firm. At a price of $1000, this producer can also supply 200 units. At the new price of $1250 the company is confident that it can supply 300 units.

9 Price elasticity of supply

4 Calculate the price elasticity of supply for the Kenyan producer of water pumps and explain what the estimate means.

5 Calculate the price elasticity of supply for the German producer of water pumps and explain what the estimate means.

6 Explain the difference in the price elasticity of supply of water pumps between the Kenyan and German producers.

7 Explain how this difference affects the ability of Kenyan and German producers to change supply.

8 Analyse how a 10% fall in the price of water pumps would affect the quantities that each producer is willing to supply.

> **TIP**
>
> Unlike measures of elasticity of demand, price elasticity of supply is always positive. An increase in price will always lead to an increase in the quantity supplied. Learners sometimes forget this when writing about price elasticity of supply.

Evaluation

9 Consider whether the Kenyan producer is correct to claim that it 'can respond quickly to price changes in the market'.

WORKED EXAMPLE FOR Q9

The data indicate that both producers can increase supply when the price *suddenly* increases, but to a varying extent. This can be shown by the calculations for price elasticity of supply. These estimates are 0.4 for the Kenyan producer and 2 for the German producer [A]. This means that the German producer is able to respond with a greater increase than the Kenyan producer [E].

10 Comment on whether there is anything either producer can do to be more responsive to a change in the price of water pumps.

PRACTICE QUESTIONS

Multiple-choice question

1 A firm supplies 500 bars of chocolate which the firm sells for $2 per bar. Due to a shortage in the market, the price increases to $2.50 per bar. The firm now sells 800 bars of chocolate. Which of these is the correct calculation and interpretation of price elasticity of supply?

A	2.4	price elastic
B	2.4	price inelastic
C	0.42	price elastic
D	0.42	price inelastic

Essay questions

1 Most agricultural products have an inelastic price elasticity of supply. Analyse how this affects the market **and** consider if anything can be done to make the supply of these products less price inelastic.

2 Explain the factors that might affect the price elasticity of supply of goods from a garment producer in Bangladesh **and** consider which factors are the most important.

CONTINUED

Improve this answer

This is a sample answer to essay Q2.

> The price elasticity of supply (PES) is the term used to measure the responsiveness of supply to a change in the price of a product. It is a numerical measure that is always positive since it is assumed that a producer will supply more when the price increases **[K]**.
>
> It can be assumed that, unlike an agricultural producer, the manufacturer of garments in Bangladesh will have a relatively elastic price elasticity of supply **[K]**. This is because there are certain ways in which the quantity of garments can be controlled depending upon the market price.
>
> The first factor that can make the PES more elastic is through building up stock and holding this in a warehouse **[K]**. Stock can be released or stored as the market price changes. If there is a surge in demand, the manufacturer has the means to meet it. In the short term, production can be increased by operating an additional shift or by getting workers to work longer hours **[A]**.
>
> A second and related factor is the time period. If a firm has spare manufacturing capacity, then this can be quickly put into production, or removed from production, if market prices change **[A]**. It will also depend on whether there are skilled workers looking for a job.
>
> There may be a third longer-term option. This would be to increase the size of the business through an expansion in capacity to produce garments. This will involve new investment and very likely, new technology **[A]**. It will also require the manufacturer to be reasonably certain that there will be a future market for these products.
>
> It is not easy to say which factor is likely to be most important **[E]**. This is because each business has its own characteristics – for some it may be to accumulate new stock, for others it may be to work longer hours **[E]**.

Your challenge

See whether you can improve this answer. The answer is written in a clear analytical style, and covers the topic in an appropriate way. The definition of PES could be supported by the formula and include a brief explanation of the difference between elastic and an inelastic supply. The second paragraph could include more detail on how an elastic supply could help the garment manufacturer. The conclusion includes some evaluation which could be developed further. A better answer is given in the workbook answers - but write yours out first.

> Chapter 10
The interaction of demand and supply

LEARNING INTENTIONS

In this chapter you will:

- define the meaning of equilibrium and disequilibrium in a market
- explain the shifts in demand and supply curves on equilibrium price and quantity
- explain the relationships between different markets, including: joint demand (complements); alternative demand (substitutes); derived demand; joint supply
- analyse the functions of price in resource allocation; signalling (transmission of preferences) and the provision of incentives (incentivising).

KEY TERMS

Ad valorem tax   Change in demand   Change in supply   Derived demand   Disequilibrium   Equilibrium
Equilibrium price   Equilibrium quantity   Excise duties   Incentive   Joint supply   Rationing   Signalling
Specific tax   Transmission of preferences

Key skills exercises

Knowledge and understanding

To answer the questions in this chapter, you need to know and understand:

- what is meant by equilibrium and disequilibrium in a market
- how shifts in demand and supply curves affect equilibrium price and quantity
- the causes of shifts in demand and supply curves
- the meaning of complements, substitutes, derived demand and joint supply
- how price acts as an allocative mechanism in markets
- signalling and the provision of incentives.

1. Define what is meant by 'equilibrium' in a market.
2. Define what is meant by 'disequilibrium' in a market.
3. Explain what is meant by equilibrium price and equilibrium quantity.
4. Explain what is meant by a change in demand and the effects on equilibrium price and quantity.
5. Explain what is meant by a change in supply and the effects on equilibrium price and quantity.
6. Explain the reasons for a shift in the demand curve.
7. Explain the reasons for a shift in the supply curve.

Analysis

Avocado inflation

In summer 2019, the price of avocados on the world market increased by over 50% in just a few weeks. Figure 10.1 shows what happened to the wholesale price of avocados produced in Mexico, the world's largest supplier, where production was believed to 'be at a maximum'. The supply was also hit by a fall in production in the USA, the world's second larger supplier. On the demand side, for health reasons, the demand for avocados has increased in recent years. This is the case in the USA, much of the European Union (EU), the UK and among China's growing middle class.

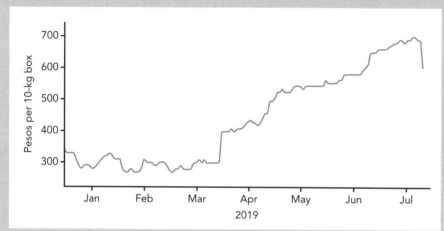

Figure 10.1: The wholesale price of avocados produced in Mexico, 2019 (in Mexican pesos)

Source: Mexican Ministry of Economy

Figure 10.2 shows how an economist would represent this situation.

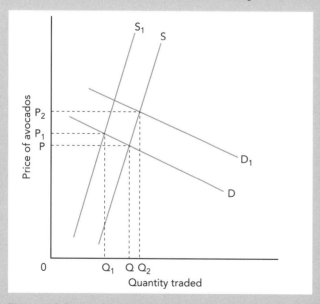

Figure 10.2: A reduction in supply and an increase in demand for avocados

10 The interaction of demand and supply

8   Explain why the market is in disequilibrium at price P and quantity Q_1.
9   Analyse how this market can return to equilibrium.
10 Explain **two** possible reasons for a fall in supply of avocados.
11 Explain **two** reasons for the increase in demand for avocados.
12 Analyse the effect of an increase in demand for avocados on price and quantity traded.
13 Analyse the effect of an increase in supply of avocados on price and quantity traded.
14 Analyse the impact on the EU market for avocados if the EU imposes a specific tax on the import of avocados from the USA.

Evaluation

15 Comment on the circumstances where an increase in supply and an increase in demand lead an increase in the quantity of avocados traded but no change in price.

PRACTICE QUESTIONS

Data response question

1   a   Using the data in Figure 10.1, describe how the price of avocados changed from January to July 2019.
    b   Calculate the approximate change in price of avocados from April to the end of June 2019.

WORKED EXAMPLE FOR Q1

a   There has been a substantial increase in the price of avocados from January to July 2019 **[K]**. The increase in price was particularly steep from April 2019 **[K]**. The price of avocados was relatively stable from January to the end of March 2019 **[K]**.

b   % change in price $= \dfrac{\text{change in price}}{\text{price in April}}$

$= \dfrac{200}{400} \times 100\%$

$= 50\%$ increase

Essay questions

1   A recent television programme in the UK claimed that fresh and ground turmeric was a new 'super food' that may provide relief from a wide range of medical problems, including depression and anxiety.
    a   With the help of a diagram, analyse how the claim is likely to have affected the market for turmeric **and** consider how certain you might be about the market outcome.
    b   Discuss whether the market might be able to respond to this claim.
2   Many governments have introduced 'sugar taxes' in order to restrict consumption of soft drinks and other products containing high amounts of sugar.
    a   With the help of a diagram, explain the effects on the market of a new specific tax on sugar **and** consider whether an *ad valorem* tax would be more suitable.
    b   Discuss whether a sugar tax is the best way of restricting the consumption of soft drinks and other products containing sugar.

> **TIP**
>
> When asked to use a diagram or when you include a diagram, make sure that you refer to the diagram in a clear way. This is a valid form of analysis.

CONTINUED

Improve this answer

This is a sample answer to essay Q1.

a The claim that turmeric helps medical problems like depression came from a recent TV programme. The effect of the TV programme will have been to increase the demand that some TV viewers have for turmeric. This can be shown by an increase in demand on the diagram **[K]**.

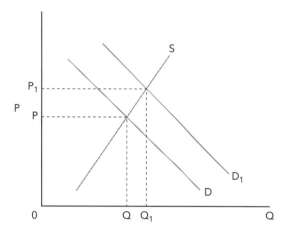

The effect on the market is that the increase in demand has resulted in an increase in quantity traded in the market but price has also increased **[A]**. The increase is shown by a movement up the supply curve.

b The market can respond to the claim. More will be demanded by consumers and this will require producers of turmeric to produce more in order to meet the increase in demand **[A]**.

In terms of supply, the pressure will be on farmers to grow more turmeric. They can sell this as fresh or they can send it to a factory for processing into turmeric powder. The producer can then supply the market. It may be that the producer also has some stocks of turmeric that have been built up **[A]**.

Another consideration is with demand. Consumers may find that because of the increased demand, the price of turmeric increases a lot and is more than they can afford to pay **[A]**. This involves the price elasticity of demand. This could be an issue for poorer families who find that similar health claims are made for other spices **[A]**.

Your challenge

See whether you can improve these answers. Both answers are short and written in a descriptive way. Neither answer contains evaluation as required by both questions. In part (a), there is no clear analysis of the diagram. In part (b), there is no reference to the price elasticity of supply although the second paragraph includes some basic supply considerations. A better answer is given in the workbook answers – but write yours out first.

> Chapter 11
Consumer and producer surplus

LEARNING INTENTIONS

In this chapter you will:

- explain the meaning and significance of consumer surplus
- explain the meaning and significance of producer surplus
- explain the causes of changes in consumer and producer surplus
- analyse the significance of price elasticity of demand and supply in determining the extent of changes in consumer and producer surplus.

KEY TERMS

Consumer surplus   Producer surplus

Key skills exercises

Knowledge and understanding

To answer the questions in this chapter, you need to know and understand:

- what is meant by consumer surplus
- how consumer surplus is measured
- how consumer surplus is represented on a diagram
- what is meant by producer surplus
- how producer surplus is measured
- how producer surplus is represented on a diagram.

1   Define the term 'consumer surplus'.
2   Define the term 'producer surplus'.

Analysis

The prices of concert tickets

Figure 11.1 shows the price and quantity traded for tickets to a concert.

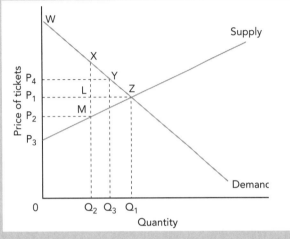

Figure 11.1: Supply and demand for concert tickets

3 What is the consumer surplus at the equilibrium position P_1Q_1?

4 Explain what happens to consumer surplus when the price of tickets increases to P_4.

5 Explain what happens to consumer surplus when the price of tickets decreases to P_2.

6 What is the producer surplus at the equilibrium position P_1Q_1?

7 Explain what happens to producer surplus when the price of tickets increases to P_4.

8 Explain what happens to producer surplus when the price of tickets decreases to P_2.

9 Analyse what happens to consumer surplus when there is a decrease in the supply of tickets.

WORKED EXAMPLE FOR Q9

A decrease in supply is represented by a shift to the left of the supply curve. This leads to an increase in the price of concert tickets and, therefore, a fall in consumer surplus [A].

10 Analyse what happens to producer surplus when there is an increase in the supply of tickets.

11 Analyse how consumer surplus changes when the demand curve becomes more price inelastic.

12 Analyse how producer surplus changes when the supply curve becomes more elastic.

TIP

The concepts of consumer surplus and producer surplus are not easy to understand. Recall the definitions. The point to remember is that consumer surplus is the price that consumers would be willing to pay and that producer surplus is the price at which producers would be willing to supply relative to the actual market prices. In each case, it is what consumers or prioducers are *willing* to pay or produce, not what actually happens.

11 Consumer and producer surplus

PRACTICE QUESTIONS

Multiple-choice question

1   Three friends meet at a restaurant. The information below shows what each of the friends is willing to pay for a meal.

Ayesha $14, Ruky $12, Neema $10

The total bill is $18, which they decide to split evenly.

How much should each of the friends pay to obtain the same consumer surplus?

	Ayesha	Ruky	Neema
A	$2	$6	$10
B	$6	$6	$6
C	$8	$6	$4
D	$10	$6	$2

Essay question

1   Explain how consumer surplus is affected by an increase in the price of a good **and** consider whether imposing a new indirect tax increases or reduces consumer surplus.

Improve this answer

This is a sample answer to essay Q1.

> Consumer surplus is when a consumer gets more for their money than they were expecting. A good example is at the supermarket. Suppose the price of a packet of rice has been reduced to $2. If the consumer was expecting to pay $3 then the consumer surplus is the difference, $1 **[K]**.
>
> If the price increases, then this is shown by a movement up and along the demand curve. In the case of rice, if the new price increases to $2.50 consumer surplus will be reduced. The consumer may then buy fewer packets of rice **[A]**.
>
> The effect of an indirect tax is to shift the supply curve to the left. This sees the price increase and the quantity supplied will fall **[A]**. The consumer surplus also falls as a result.

Your challenge

See whether you can improve this answer. The answer is too short and lacks some precision. The definition is weak. The answer would be improved if it included a diagram. The final paragraph needs more analysis and also some evaluation to make clear whether the new indirect tax actually increases or decreases consumer surplus.. A better answer is given in the workbook answers – but write yours out first.

Unit 3
Government microeconomic intervention (AS Level)

> Chapter 12
Reasons for government intervention in markets

LEARNING INTENTIONS

In this chapter you will:

- explain why there is the non-provision of public goods
- explain why there is overconsumption of demerit goods and the underconsumption of merit goods
- explain why governments control prices in markets.

KEY TERM

Market failure

Key skills exercises

Knowledge and understanding

To answer the questions in this chapter, you need to know and understand:

- why market failure requires government intervention
- why there is non-provision of public goods
- why information failure leads to the over-consumption of demerit goods and the under-consumption of merit goods
- how governments control prices in some markets.

1 Define the term 'market failure'.
2 Justify **three** examples of market failure.
3 Explain why governments provide public goods.
4 Explain why demerit goods are over-consumed in a free market.
5 Explain why merit goods are under-consumed in a free market.
6 Describe **three** ways in which a government can control prices in an economy.

12 Reasons for government intervention in markets

Analysis

> **Increasing restrictions on smoking tobacco products**
>
> There was a time when it was fashionable to be seen smoking a cigarette. This is no longer the case. Many countries have now banned smoking in public places and added other restrictions on the sale and consumption of tobacco products.
>
> In 2004, Bhutan was the first country not only to ban smoking in public places but to also ban the sale of tobacco. It did this in order to raise its ranking in the Gross National Happiness Index.
>
> In Malaysia, smoking is now banned in airports, restaurants, public toilets, government premises and private offices. If anyone is found smoking in a private office where the building has air conditioning, there could be a large fine of up to 10 000 Malaysian ringgits (approximately $2350).
>
> The UK has been at the forefront of anti-smoking legislation to support the ban on smoking in public places including:
>
> - an increase from age 16 to 18 at which tobacco products can be purchased
> - picture warnings on cigarette packets
> - a ban on tobacco displays in large stores
> - standardised (plain) packaging for cigarettes (this was first introduced in Australia).

7 Explain why smoking in public places is a demerit good.

8 Analyse how opportunity cost can be applied to a government's decision to fund measures to restrict consumption of tobacco products.

9 How might a government control the price of tobacco products?

Evaluation

10 Consider why it has been necessary for the UK government to require standardised packaging for cigarettes.

11 Comment on the criteria an economist might use to assess whether restricting the sale and use of tobacco products has been effective.

WORKED EXAMPLE FOR Q11

A good approach is to use cost–benefit analysis **[K]**. Some inputs are:

- Benefits: healthier population, less absenteeism from work, increased economic growth, better social environment, less pressure on healthcare services
- Costs: loss of tax revenue to government, cost of applying regulations, jobs lost in tobacco industry and some leisure services such as bars and restaurants. **[A]**.

It is not easy to apply these criteria, as past information is unlikely to be available **[E]**.

CAMBRIDGE INTERNATIONAL AS & A LEVEL ECONOMICS: WORKBOOK

PRACTICE QUESTIONS

Multiple-choice question

1   Not all goods and services provided by the public sector are classified as 'public goods'.
    Why is this?

    A   There is a limit to government funding for public goods.

    B   It is not possible to control 'free-riders'.

    C   Some goods and services can be provided by both public and private sectors.

    D   The public sector is not aware of what goods and services it should provide.

Essay questions

1   Discuss why it is often necessary for governments to provide goods and services.
2   Explain the difference between private goods and merit goods, **and** consider why a government only intervenes in the case of merit goods.

Improve this answer

This is a sample answer to essay Q1.

> In all types of economy it is necessary for its government to provide certain goods and services. This is because private enterprise is unwilling or possibly unable to do so **[K]**.
>
> A good example is that of government provision of public goods such as a police force, roads, flood control systems and even lighthouses in some coastal areas. For such services, it is not possible or practical for the private sector to provide them **[A]**. An exception is a toll road, but in the case of the other services, it is totally impractical to charge for them at what is the 'point of use'.
>
> Take the case of the fire service in most cities. This is a government-funded service paid for out of tax revenue. When there is an incident, it is absurd to suggest that the fire officer asks for your credit card before they will attempt to put out the fire **[K]**.
>
> Central to the context is the matter of 'free riders' when it comes to public goods. This is the term used to describe someone who benefits from using a public good, but who has not contributed any money towards its continuing operation **[A]**.
>
> To conclude, it is very clear that it is essential for governments to provide public goods despite the obvious inequities arising from free riders. If they were not to produce such goods, then they would not be provided by the private sector as it would not be viable or feasible for them to do so **[E]**.

Your challenge

See whether you can improve this answer. The answer has the potential to be an even better answer. The main omission is that it does not consider issues relating to merit goods and the direct provision of services such as healthcare and education. See if you can add another two paragraphs following paragraph 4, and also rewrite the final paragraph to make it more evaluative. This should give a much more complete answer. A better answer is given in the workbook answers – but write yours out first.

Chapter 13
Methods and effects of government intervention in markets

LEARNING INTENTIONS

In this chapter you will:

- analyse the impact and incidence of specific indirect taxes
- analyse the impact and incidence of subsidies
- explain direct provision of goods and services
- analyse maximum and minimum prices
- analyse buffer stock schemes
- explain provision of information.

KEY TERMS

Buffer stock scheme   Incidence   Maximum price   Minimum price   Subsidies

Key skills exercises

Knowledge and understanding

To answer the questions in this chapter, you need to know and understand:

- the difference between *ad valorem* and specific taxes
- the extent to which the incidence of an indirect tax is borne by the producer or the consumer or by both
- the effects of a subsidy on a market
- why governments directly provide some goods and services
- the effects of minimum and maximum price controls on a market
- how a buffer stock scheme works.

1. Define an *ad valorem* tax and give an example.
2. Define a specific tax and give an example.
3. Explain what is meant by the incidence of an indirect tax.
4. Describe what is meant by a subsidy.
5. Explain how a subsidy affects the price and quantity traded in a market.
6. Explain how maximum price works in a market and give an example.

Analysis

Myanmar government backs minimum price for rice

The Myanmar government fixed the minimum price for rice at 500 000 kyats for 100 baskets of paddy ($327 for about 2 tons) in October 2019. The government set a minimum price so as to establish a fair market price for the country's paddy farmers.

Under the scheme, the government paid the farmer the minimum price, but only if the paddy was of good quality. If the market price rose above the floor price, then the rice would be bought and sold at the market rate. If the market price fell below the floor price, then the government would buy the paddy at the agreed floor price.

The farmer's union welcomed the new minimum price, while taking the view that it could have been higher. Figure 13.1 shows how this situation can be represented in economic theory.

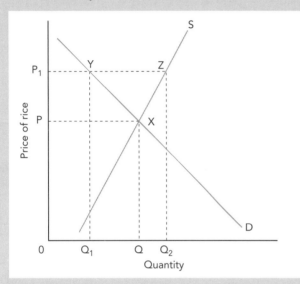

Figure 13.1: A minimum price for rice

7 Using Figure 13.1:
    a   What is the equilibrium price and quantity?
    b   If the minimum price is P_1, how much is supplied and demanded?
    c   What is the surplus in the market?

8   Analyse how the market for rice might return to an equilibrium position.

9   Explain what would happen to the market for rice if the maximum price was below the equilibrium price.

Evaluation

10   Discuss which groups are likely to benefit and which groups are likely to lose out as a result of a minimum price for rice being introduced in Myanmar.

13 Methods and effects of government intervention in markets

> **WORKED EXAMPLE FOR Q10**
>
> Farmers will benefit from higher prices for rice. This is the main reason for the introduction of a minimum price **[K]**. Consumers are likely to lose out due to the higher price of rice, although they will benefit from secure supplies **[K]**. The government will have to offset the cost of the subsidy against not having to import rice from elsewhere in Asia. It will also be necessary for the government to buy up excess supplies of rice **[A]**.

11 Comment upon any wider global resource implications of introducing a minimum price for agricultural products in Myanmar.

PRACTICE QUESTIONS

Multiple-choice question

1 In which of the situations below is the consumer most likely to pay a greater proportion of the tax burden than the producer?

	Type of indirect tax	Price elasticity of demand
A	ad valorem	inelastic
B	ad valorem	elastic
C	specific	inelastic
D	specific	elastic

Essay questions

1 Explain whether it is feasible to charge a maximum price for basic foodstuffs for low-income families.

2 Discuss whether all forms of passenger transport (mass transit) should be subsidised by the government of a middle-income economy.

3 In April 2018, South Africa became the latest of a growing list of countries to introduce a sugar tax on cans of soft drinks. Other countries have rejected such taxes.

   a Explain how the sugar tax is likely to affect the market for cans of soft drinks in South Africa **and** consider how the tax might be most effective.

   b Discuss why some countries have introduced sugar taxes while other countries have rejected the idea.

> **TIP**
>
> Note the wording of Q2 and Q3. It is asking for some evaluation in your answers. Questions in other chapters may say 'consider' when asking for evaluation.

CAMBRIDGE INTERNATIONAL AS & A LEVEL ECONOMICS: WORKBOOK

CONTINUED

Improve this answer

This is a sample answer to essay Q2.

A subsidy is a payment that is usually made by a government to a producer of a good or service **[K]**. In this case it is paid to various forms of passenger transport. By definition, passenger transport includes buses, railways, aeroplanes and in some countries like mine, tuk tuks.

The diagram below shows the impact of introducing a subsidy in a market. A subsidy shifts the supply curve to the right, meaning more will be supplied at the new lower subsidised price **[K]**.

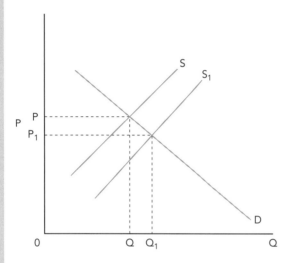

The main point about a subsidy is that it reduces the price to consumers. This will be very beneficial to those on low incomes, although the subsidy in general will reduce the fares of all passengers on a bus **[A]**. The same will be true of an urban railway or tram system.

Another reason why big cities subsidise public transport is that it can help to reduce congestion on the roads. The purpose is just this and will produce a more efficient transport system **[A]**. The system will also be more sustainable since air pollution will be reduced.

A third major benefit is that subsidised public transport services are likely to make it cheaper for workers, especially low-paid ones, to get a job. Cheaper fares also widen the geographical possibilities for employment **[A]**.

One of the main criticisms of any subsidised service is the cost to whoever is providing the subsidy, in most cases the government. There are opportunity cost considerations, especially in situations where public funding is limited. A further criticism is that many travellers can afford to pay the full market price rather than the subsidised price of travel **[E]**.

Your challenge

See whether you can improve this answer. The answer has some content which can be developed. There are some weaknesses. More use could be made of the diagram through using it to explain how a subsidy works. The only indication of application to middle-income countries is a hint through the use of some examples. This needs to be developed. The answer would benefit from a better conclusion that ends with a clear statement as to whether all forms of public transport should be subsidised. A better answer is given in the workbook answers – but write yours out first.

Chapter 14
Addressing income and wealth inequality

LEARNING INTENTIONS

In this chapter you will:

- explain the difference between income as a flow concept and wealth as a stock concept
- measure inequality in income and wealth with a Gini coefficient
- explain the economic reasons for inequality in income and wealth
- discuss policies that redistribute income and wealth, including the minimum wage, transfer payments, progressive income taxes, inheritance and capital taxes, and state provision of essential goods and services.

KEY TERMS

Capital tax   Gini coefficient   Informal economy   Inheritance tax   Minimum wage   Progressive tax
Transfer payment   Wealth

Key skills exercises

Knowledge and understanding

To answer the questions in this chapter, you need to know and understand:

- the difference between income and wealth
- what is measured by the Gini coefficient
- the economic reasons for inequality in income and wealth
- policies that are able to redistribute income and wealth.

> **TIP**
>
> Many learners confuse income and wealth. Remember that income is a *flow* of payments over time, whereas wealth is a *stock* of assets (including money) at a point in time.

1   Describe the difference between income and wealth.
2   Describe what is measured by a Gini coefficient.
3   Explain the significance of extreme values of 0 and 1 for a Gini coefficient.
4   Explain the difference between the formal part of an economy and the informal (hidden) part of an economy.
5   Explain the purpose of a minimum wage rate.
6   Describe what is meant by a transfer payment and give an example.
7   Explain the features of a progressive tax system.
8   Explain **two** examples of taxes that can reduce inequalities in the distribution of wealth.

Analysis

Income inequality in Vietnam

Vietnam is a middle-income country with a mainly socialist economy. A series of economic and social reforms, known as Doi Moi, have been responsible for transforming Vietnam's economy from being one of the poorest in Southeast Asia to one that has experienced substantial growth over the past 30 years.

The 'economic miracle' though has not benefited all of the country's 95m population. Income inequality has increased, especially among ethnic minorities, small farmers, migrant workers and women. Figure 14.1 shows the extent of income equality in 2018.

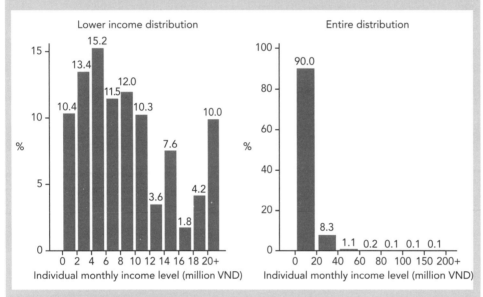

VND: the dong is the currency of Vietnam.

Figure 14.1: Monthly income distribution, Vietnam, 2018

Source: Vietnam Provincial Governance and Public Administration Performance Index (PAPI) report

A recent report by Oxfam has estimated that the richest person in Vietnam earns more in a day than the poorest Vietnamese person earns in 10 years. In terms of wealth, this rich person could spend $1m every day for six years before exhausting their wealth.

Oxfam believes that income inequality is holding back Vietnam's otherwise healthy economic progress. The problem requires a more progressive tax bracket for billionaires, improved public services and better workers' rights. Only in this way can Vietnam's economic miracle benefit many millions more than is the case at present.

9   Analyse the likely economic reasons why income inequality among certain groups in the population of Vietnam has increased.

10 With the help of a diagram, analyse how a progressive income tax system can improve the distribution of income in Vietnam.

11 Analyse how improved public services can reduce inequalities in income in Vietnam.

14 Addressing income and wealth inequality

Evaluation

12 Assess why it is believed that increasing income and wealth inequality could hold back Vietnam's economic progress.

PRACTICE QUESTIONS

Data response question

1 The Gini coefficient for Vietnam in 2018 was 0.307. Using the data in Figure 14.1, does this coefficient seem to be a fair estimate of Vietnam's income inequality?

> **WORKED EXAMPLE FOR Q1**
>
> The low value of the Gini coefficient appears to be consistent with the data in Figure 14.1. 90% of the population are in the lowest income band. Within this band around 60% are in the bottom half of the band. The percentage of people in the top bands is insignificant **[A]**.

Essay question

1 Explain which types of tax might improve the distribution of income in a country **and** consider **one** tax that can be most easily applied in a lower middle-income country.

Improve this answer

This is a sample answer to essay Q1.

> A tax is a payment that is made by individuals to the government. It can be in the form of a regular weekly or monthly payment that is taken out of wages, or it can be an immediate payment that is included in the price of goods and services such as petrol, restaurant meals, sugary soft drinks and so on. The main purpose of taxation is to fund government spending on education, healthcare, roads, transfer payments to the poor and so on **[K]**.
>
> In terms of improving the distribution of income, a regressive tax system is best. Rich people tend to buy more valuable goods and services than poor people. They therefore pay more taxation to the government when they buy expensive cars, clothes and jewellery or go on exotic holidays to Australia and Europe. In contrast poor people have low incomes and are not in a position to contribute much money in the form of taxation.
>
> There are also progressive taxes like income tax. High earners obviously pay more income tax than workers on a minimum wage. These workers will not pay any income tax at all on their low wages. Although higher earners pay more tax, the total tax paid is low and much less than is being generated from taxes such as general sales tax. This is because only a small percentage of workers actually pay income tax. There is also the issue of the informal economy to consider. It can therefore be concluded that a regressive tax system is by far the best system for reducing income inequality, since it generates the biggest sums of money for the government to put into policies to improve the well-being of the poorest people and therefore the distribution of income.

Your challenge

See whether you can improve this answer. The answer is very poor. The first paragraph is sufficient on the purpose of taxation. Little else in the answer is correct or relevant. In particular, the learner does not understand the difference between a progressive tax system and a regressive tax system. This is a fundamental factual error which makes the answer meaningless. There is no explicit attempt to apply the answer to a lower middle-income country. A better answer is given in the workbook answers – but write yours out first.

› Unit 4
The macroeconomy (AS Level)

> Chapter 15
National income statistics

LEARNING INTENTIONS

In this chapter you will:

- define the meaning of national income
- explain the purpose of national income statistics
- explain the difference between gross domestic product (GDP), gross national income (GNI) and net national income (NNI)
- analyse the three methods of measuring GDP
- explain how measures of national income are adjusted from market prices to basic prices
- explain how measures of national income are adjusted from gross values to net values.

KEY TERMS

Basic prices   Compensation of employees   Depreciation   Expenditure method
Gross domestic product (GDP)   Gross investment   Gross national disposable income   Gross national income (GNI)
Income method   Market prices   Multinational companies (MNCs)   National income
National income statistics   Net domestic product (NDP)   Net investment   Net national income (NNI)
Net property income from abroad   Output method   Value added

Key skills exercises

Knowledge and understanding

To answer the questions in this chapter, you need to know and understand:

- what is meant by GDP
- the differences between GDP, GNI and NNI
- the meaning of net property income from abroad and how it is calculated
- the difference between net income from abroad and net property income from abroad
- the three ways in which GDP can be measured
- how measures of national income are adjusted from market prices to basic prices
- how measures of national income are adjusted from gross values to net values
- issues associated with collecting national income data.

TIP

When using national income statistics, be careful to note whether the data is measured in US dollars or local currency and when the data was compiled. This is especially important when making comparisons.

1   What do national income statistics measure?
2   Define GDP.

15 National income statistics

3   What is the difference between GDP and GNI?
4   What is the difference between GNI and NNI?
5   What is net property income from abroad?
6   Explain the difference between net income from abroad and net property income from abroad.
7   Explain the **three** ways in which GDP is measured.

WORKED EXAMPLE FOR Q7

GDP can be measured in three ways. These are known as the output, income and expenditure methods. The output method measures the value of goods and services produced in each of the industries or sectors of the economy. These industries include agriculture, mining, manufacturing, transport, retail and so on. The income method is based on income that is paid to factors of production that produce an economy's output. The sources of income are wages, rent, interest and profit. The expenditure method adds up spending by households and governments plus investment expenditure and net exports **[K]**.

8   How are measures of national income adjusted from market prices to basic prices?
9   How are measures of national income adjusted from gross values to net values?

Analysis

National income statistics, Pakistan

Table 15.1 shows two key national income statistics for Pakistan in 2019. Table 15.2 shows the composition of gross domestic product by sector for Pakistan in 2018.

	$ (millions)
Gross domestic product (GDP)	284 210
Gross national income (GNI)	331 364

Table 15.1: Key national income statistics, Pakistan, 2019

	Pakistani rupees (millions)
Gross domestic product (constant prices)	13 100
GDP from agriculture	2336
GDP from construction	343
GDP from manufacturing	1666
GDP from mining	344
GDP from services	7423
GDP from transport	1591

Note: the sector data is not equal to total GDP due to incomplete data.
Table 15.2: Composition of gross domestic product by sector, Pakistan, 2018.

10 Calculate Pakistan's net property income from abroad in 2019.
11 Calculate Pakistan's net income from abroad in 2019.
12 Analyse the relative importance of the composition of Pakistan's GDP in 2018.

Evaluation

13 Comment on some of the problems of collecting data for estimating GDP in different types of economy.

PRACTICE QUESTIONS

Data response question

1   The following table shows information from the 2019 national accounts of Mauritius.

	Mauritian rupees (billions)
GDP market prices	503
GDP basic prices	440
Final consumers' expenditure	455.2
Investment	99.6
Imports of goods and services	269.8
Exports of goods and services	197.1

a   Calculate the net receipts from taxes on products and subsidies.
b   Calculate government spending on goods and services.
c   Discuss whether the Mauritian government should be concerned about its balance of trade in goods and services.

Essay question

1   Explain **one** way gross domestic product (GDP) is calculated **and** consider whether the estimates are likely to be more accurate in a high-income country than in a lower-income country.

Improve this answer

This is a sample answer to essay Q1.

> Gross domestic product, or GDP as it is known, measures the total output produced in an economy over one year. It can be measured in three ways: the output, income and expenditure methods **[K]**.
>
> The output method calculates the value of output produced by all of the industries in the economy. This includes farming and services such as power supply, banking and transport as well as manufacturing industry. The last industry, as well as agriculture, produce goods whose value to the economy can be measured **[K]**. It is much more difficult in the case of service industries.

15 National income statistics

> **CONTINUED**
>
> In a high income country such as the USA and the UK, measuring output is easier than in a low income country. This is because virtually all that is produced reaches the market and so can be given a monetary value. In a lower income country, where agriculture is likely to be an important activity, measuring output is much more difficult. This is because many farmers operate on a subsistence basis, with little or nothing that they produce being sent to market. These are also likely to be barter transactions, and corruption which makes estimating production difficult. The absence of a monetarised market is also likely to affect other sectors such as construction and small-scale manufacturing **[E]**.
>
> So it would seem most likely that estimates of GDP will be more accurate in a high-income country than in one which has a low income **[E]**.
>
> **Your challenge**
>
> See whether you can improve this answer. This is a clearly written answer with a logical structure. The final two paragraphs contain relevant evaluation. The explanation of the output method in the second paragraph is limited. The answer needs a new second paragraph containing a more detailed explanation of the output method. A better answer is given in the workbook answers – but write yours out first.

Chapter 16
Introduction to the circular flow of income

LEARNING INTENTIONS

In this chapter you will:

- define the circular flow of income
- explain the difference between the circular flow of income in a closed economy and in an open economy: the flow of income between households, firms and the government and the international economy
- analyse the impact of injections and leakages on the circular flow of income
- identify the difference between the country's income being in equilibrium and being in disequilibrium.

KEY TERMS

Circular flow of income model   Closed economy   Injections   Leakages   Open economy

Key skills exercises

Knowledge and understanding

To answer the questions in this chapter, you need to know and understand:

- what is meant by the circular flow of income
- the difference between an open economy and a closed economy
- how the circular flow of income can be represented in a simple diagram
- the difference between the circular flow of income in a closed economy and in an open economy
- how a change in injections or leakages affects the equilibrium of the circular flow of income
- how to determine when a country's income is in equilibrium or disequilibrium.

1 Draw a simple model of the circular flow of income in an economy.
2 What is the difference between a closed economy and an open economy?
3 Draw a model of the circular flow of income in an open economy.
4 Describe what is meant by an injection into the circular flow of income.
5 Give **three** examples of injections into the circular flow of income of an open economy.
6 Describe what is meant by a leakage from the circular flow of income.
7 Give **three** examples of leakages from the circular flow of income of an open economy.
8 Explain the equilibrium income in a two-sector economy.
9 Explain the equilibrium level of income in a four-sector economy.

> ### TIP
>
> A common mistake is for learners to mix up injections with withdrawals. A useful way of avoiding this mistake is to imagine a tap over a bucket. Turning on the tap (injection) increases water in the bucket (income). A hole in the bucket (leakage) reduces water in the bucket (income).

Analysis

Output growth in Mauritius

Mauritius has experienced output growth of 3–4% since 2016. The service sector, which includes retailing, financial services and the provision of accommodation and food services, has been the main contributor to this growth, mainly through the services provided for international tourists.

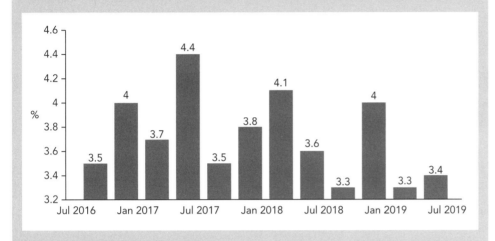

Figure 16.1: Quarterly percentage change in GDP for Mauritius, July 2016–July 2019

Source: Central Statistics Office, Mauritius

10 Justify **two** examples of injections into the circular flow of income in Mauritius.

11 Justify **two** examples of leakages from the circular flow of income in Mauritius.

12 Analyse how a reduction in income taxes affects the circular flow of income in Mauritius.

13 Analyse how an increase in government spending on the country's ports affects the circular flow of income in Mauritius.

WORKED EXAMPLE FOR Q13

An increase in government spending on ports is an injection into the circular flow of income **[K]**. This additional spending will lead to increased spending by workers employed on the port project. There is also likely to be new investment by private sector firms. Over time, increased spending on ports could attract more cruise vessels to dock in Mauritius. So, over time, there will be an increase in the circular flow of income **[A]**.

PRACTICE QUESTIONS

Data response question

1   a   Use Figure 16.1 to describe the quarterly change in the growth rate of Mauritius from July 2016 to July 2019.
    b   Comment on how seasonal fluctuations affect the circular flow of income in Mauritius.

Essay question

1   Analyse how a sudden decrease in the number of international tourists leads to disequilibrium in the circular flow of income in an economy **and** consider how a decrease could be avoided.

Improve this answer

This is a sample answer to essay Q1.

> International tourists are an important source of income for many economies. Some of these economies have few other sources of income. The income gained from international tourists is an export in the same way as if the economy were selling agricultural goods overseas **[K]**.
>
> The money spent by international tourists provides an income for those people working in hotels, restaurants, bars, shops and tourist attractions. These people are consumers, and will spend a large proportion of their income on consumption **[A]**. This increases the circular flow of income.
>
> A decrease in the number of international tourists will cause disequilibrium in the circular flow of income. Leakages will increase and the level of income in the economy will fall **[A]**.
>
> The sudden decrease is likely to have been caused by an external shock, over which the economy receiving tourists will have no control **[E]**. This shock is likely to cause a fall in incomes with a reduction in demand for international travel.

Your challenge

See whether you can improve this answer. The answer meets the requirements of the question although it could be enhanced with a diagram of the circular flow of income in an open economy. The diagram is best placed between the second and third paragraphs of the answer. Your challenge is to draw the diagram – remember to include a short paragraph to explain the diagram. A better answer is given in the workbook answers – but write yours out first.

Chapter 17
Aggregate demand and aggregate supply analysis

LEARNING INTENTIONS

In this chapter you will:

- define the meaning of aggregate demand (AD)
- explain the components of aggregate demand
- analyse the determinants of aggregate demand
- explain the shape of the aggregate demand curve
- analyse the causes of a shift in the aggregate demand curve
- define the meaning of aggregate supply (AS)
- analyse the determinants of aggregate supply
- explain the shape of the AS curve in the short run (SRAS) and long run (LRAS)
- explain the causes of a shift in the AS curve in the short run (SRAS) and in the long run (LRAS)
- identify the difference between a movement along and a shift in aggregate demand and aggregate supply
- explain how equilibrium is established in the AD/AS model and how the level of real output, the price level and employment are determined
- discuss the effects of shifts in the AD curve and the AS curve on the level of real output, the price level and employment.

KEY TERMS

Aggregate demand (AD)   Aggregate supply (AS)   Consumer expenditure   Disposable income
Dissaving   Exchange rate   Government spending   Investment   Keynesians   Long-run aggregate supply (LRAS)
Macroeconomic equilibrium   Net exports   New classical economists   Saving   Short-run aggregate supply (SRAS)
Supply-side shocks

Key skills exercises

Knowledge and understanding

To answer the questions in this chapter, you need to know and understand:

- the components of aggregate demand
- the determinants of the components of aggregate demand
- the shape of the aggregate demand curve
- the meaning of aggregate supply
- the determinants of aggregate supply
- how to distinguish between the short-run and long-run aggregate supply curves

- causes of a shift in the short-run and long-run aggregate supply curves
- the difference between a movement along and a shift in the AD and AS curves
- when the AD/AS model is in equilibrium and how this determines the level of real output, the price level and employment
- the effects of shifts in the AD and AS curves on the level of real output, the price level and employment.

1 State the **four** components of aggregate demand.
2 Describe what determines each of the components of aggregate demand.
3 Explain the shape of the aggregate demand curve.
4 Explain the difference between a movement along an AD curve and a shift of the AD curve.
5 Define aggregate supply.
6 Describe the difference between the SRAS curve and the LRAS curve.
7 Explain what causes a shift in the SRAS curve.
8 Explain what causes a shift in the LRAS curve.

Analysis

Aggregate demand in Namibia in 2018

Category of spending	Namibian dollars (millions)
Consumer spending	87 400
Gross fixed capital formation	19 971
Government spending	27 927
Exports	54 354
Imports	....
Balance of trade	−21 456

Table 17.1: Total expenditure in Namibia in 2018

Namibia's GDP fell by 0.1% in 2018, an improvement on 2017 when GDP fell by 0.9%. Despite this, consumer spending increased although government spending and spending on capital goods were both down. The main reason for the improved balance of trade figure was a 13% increase in exports. Imports were unchanged.

In August 2019, the expansion of the Walvis Bay port project was completed. This now makes Walvis Bay the preferred port for southern and central African logistics operations on the West Coast of the continent. This will benefit Namibia's own trade as it is no longer necessary for cargo to go via South Africa.

17 Aggregate demand and aggregate supply analysis

9 Explain how the fall in government spending in Namibia affects the other components of aggregate demand.

10 Analyse how the increase in exports in Namibia in 2018 affects the other components of aggregate demand.

11 With the help of a diagram, analyse how the Walvis Bay port project has affected aggregate demand in Namibia.

12 With the help of a diagram, analyse how the Walvis Bay port project has affected long-run aggregate supply in Namibia.

Evaluation

13 Assess the effects of an outward shift in the AD curve and the long-run AS curve on the level of real output, the price level and employment in Namibia.

> **TIP**
>
> When drawing aggregate demand and aggregate supply diagrams, remember to label the axes correctly. The axes should be real GDP (horizontal or x axis) and price level (vertical or y axis). A common mistake is to label the axes 'quantity' and 'price'.

PRACTICE QUESTIONS

Data response questions

1 Using the data in Table 17.1:
   a Calculate spending on imports in Namibia in 2018.
   b Calculate aggregate demand in Namibia in 2018.

2 The Walvis Bay project has been funded by the Namibian government and the African Development Bank. In which of the categories of spending shown in Table 17.1 would this expenditure be placed?

WORKED EXAMPLES FOR Q1 AND Q2

1 a Balance of trade = Exports − Imports

   $-21\,456 = 54\,354 -$ Imports

   Imports $= 54\,354 + 21\,456$

   $\quad\quad\quad = 75\,810$ (NAD m)

   b AD $= C + I + G + (X - M)$

   $\quad\quad = 87\,400 + 19\,971 + 27\,927 + (54\,354 - 75\,810)$

   $\quad\quad = 113\,842$ (NAD m)

2 It could be in both gross fixed capital formation or government spending, depending on whether the funding is from the private sector or the Namibian government.

Essay questions

1 Discuss whether a change in aggregate demand or a change in aggregate supply in an economy is likely to cause a higher level of inflation.

2 Explain the impact on aggregate supply of a reduction in taxes on firms **and** consider why there may not be an increase in real output.

3 Discuss whether an increase in long-run aggregate supply is likely to be beneficial for an economy.

CONTINUED

Improve this answer

This is a sample answer to essay Q3.

Aggregate supply is the total output that is produced in an economy. The long run is the time period when all factors of production in the economy can be changed. So long-run aggregate supply is the total output produced when any changes that have been made have had a full opportunity to come about **[K]**.

For any economy, there are many reasons why the LRAS can increase. A good current example is Qatar, where thousands of migrant workers are being employed to produce new facilities that are needed for Qatar's economic development **[A]**. They increase the size of the labour force and, in turn, total output of the economy.

A second labour consideration is where more women join the labour force, often as a result of a relaxation in attitudes towards women in work. Potentially this increases total output in the economy **[A]**.

The effects of an increase in the LRAS are shown in the diagram below.

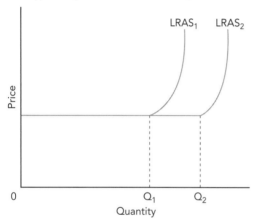

The LRAS can shift outwards for other reasons, including the discovery of new valuable mineral resources, new investment by firms and by the government in roads, railways, flood defences and power supplies and through privatisation **[A]**.

Overall, an increase in LRAS must be beneficial for an economy, as the economy's output increases. This will lead to an increase in employment **[E]**. The only negative aspect would be if it resulted in the price level increasing if the increase in LRAS has also generated an increase in aggregate demand **[E]**.

Your challenge

See whether you can improve this answer. This answer can be improved in four ways. Firstly, the definition of aggregate supply is weak. Secondly, there is no explicit reference to the diagram (note the errors here). Thirdly, the non-labour examples of how the LRAS curve shifts could be explained further. Fourthly, and significantly, there is no indication that the quality as well as the quantity of resources is important. A better answer is given in the workbook answers – but write yours out first.

Chapter 18
Economic growth

LEARNING INTENTIONS

In this chapter you will:

- define the meaning of economic growth
- describe how economic growth is measured
- explain the difference between growth in nominal GDP and real GDP
- analyse the causes of economic growth
- discuss the consequences of economic growth.

KEY TERMS

Base year   Constant prices   Economic development   Economic growth   GDP deflator
Nominal (or money) GDP   Price index   Real GDP

Key skills exercises

Knowledge and understanding

To answer the questions in this chapter, you need to know and understand:

- the meaning of economic growth
- how economic growth is measured
- how to recognise the difference between nominal GDP and real GDP
- the causes of economic growth
- the consequences of economic growth.

1. Define economic growth.
2. Describe the difference between economic growth and economic development.
3. Explain how economic growth is measured.
4. Explain the difference between nominal GDP and real GDP.
5. Explain the difference between actual and potential economic growth.

TIP

Many learners think economic growth and economic development are the same. The terms are related, but economic development is now seen as broader than economic growth. Economic development is concerned with the process of improving the economic well-being and quality of life of residents in an economy. Economic growth is narrower in scope – it is about an increase in an economy's output and productive potential.

Analysis

Nigeria's 'muted' economic growth

Year	% Annual change in GDP
2009	8.0
2010	8.0
2011	5.3
2012	4.2
2013	6.7
2014	6.3
2015	2.7
2016	−1.6
2017	0.8
2018	1.9
2019	2.3

Table 18.1: GDP growth in Nigeria, 2009–19

With a population of over 200m people, Nigeria is a key regional player in West Africa. It is the continent's biggest oil exporter and has the largest natural gas reserves in Africa.

Since 2009, Nigeria's economic growth has been variable, mainly due to the volatility in global oil prices. The price of oil collapsed in 2014 and together with a decline in manufacturing, led to the country's first recession since the early 1990s.

According to the World Bank, Nigeria's economic growth remains 'muted' (subdued). Growth is heavily dependent on the service sector, especially construction where there are a number of long-term major projects taking place. Agricultural growth remains weak, but can be improved if it is export-driven. The oil sector remains stable.

A major problem is that growth is forecast to grow more slowly than the population.

6 Analyse the causes of economic growth in Nigeria.

WORKED EXAMPLE FOR Q6

The information about Nigeria suggests three causes of the country's recent economic growth. Firstly, the service sector, and construction in particular, seem to be the main source of growth. There are long-term major projects underway. These are a form of investment and are likely to be funded by private as well as government sectors. Their construction will create new jobs, and in the future lead to an increased rate of economic growth. The second source of growth is agriculture. There appear to be opportunities for Nigerian farmers to sell their products elsewhere. This is referred to as 'export-led growth'. Finally, there is oil which has been the main cause of Nigeria's past economic growth. The information does not state just how much future growth still depends on oil [A].

18 Economic growth

7 Analyse the likely consequences of Nigeria's reduced rate of economic growth since 2014.

8 Analyse the benefits and costs of economic growth to the people of Nigeria.

Evaluation

9 Discuss whether economic development in Nigeria is improving economic well-being.

10 Comment on the World Bank's view that economic growth in Nigeria remains 'muted'.

PRACTICE QUESTIONS

Data response question

1 Using the data in Table 18.1:
  a Is the data nominal data or real data? Justify your answer.
  b Explain what evidence there is in the data to indicate that the collapse of oil prices in 2014 led to recession in Nigeria's economy?

Essay questions

1 Explain how a production possibility curve can be used to show how an economy can both develop and grow, **and** consider whether economic development or economic growth is likely to be more beneficial to the economy's population.

2 Discuss the criteria economists use when assessing the benefits and costs of economic growth in an economy.

Improve this answer

This is a sample answer to essay Q1.

The diagram below shows a production possibility curve (PPC). The axes have been labelled as consumer goods and capital goods, since an increase in consumer goods production is more likely to benefit the economy's population than if more capital goods are produced **[K]**.

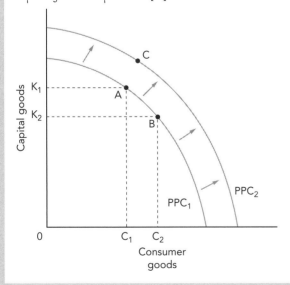

CONTINUED

Economic development can be defined as a process whereby the economic well-being and quality of life of people in an economy improves **[K]**. This can be shown to be a movement along the PPC from A to B. At B, there has been an increase in the amount of consumer goods produced from C_1 to C_2. The consequence is that the production of capital goods has decreased from K_1 to K_2. As more consumer goods are available, the well-being and quality of life of people will be improved **[A]**.

Economic growth occurs when there is an increase in an economy's output. On the diagram, this is shown by an outward shift of the PPC to PPC_2. More of each of the two types of good are now available to the economy's population. As this includes more consumer goods, it follows that the population now has an improved level of well-being **[A]**.

It is difficult to say which of these two options is likely to be more beneficial.

Your challenge

See whether you can improve this answer. This is a clear answer to the first part of the question but it does not address the evaluation issue. The last sentence could be the final evaluation, but it has no weight since it is not justified. Your challenge is to write an improved final paragraph. A better answer is given in the workbook answers – but write yours out first.

Chapter 19
Unemployment

LEARNING INTENTIONS

In this chapter you will:

- define the meaning of unemployment
- explain the difference between the economically active and economically inactive population
- explain the difference between the level of unemployment and the rate of unemployment
- calculate the rate of unemployment
- explain how unemployment is measured
- consider the difficulties of measuring unemployment
- analyse the causes and types of unemployment: frictional, structural, cyclical, seasonal and technological
- discuss the consequences of unemployment.

KEY TERMS

Casual unemployment   Claimant count measure   Cyclical unemployment   Discouraged workers
Economically active   Economically inactive   Employment rate   Frictional unemployment   Homemakers
International unemployment   Labour force   Labour force participation rate   Labour force survey measure
Level of unemployment   Regional unemployment   Sampling error   Search unemployment
Seasonal unemployment   Structural unemployment   Technological unemployment
Underemployment   Unemployment   Unemployment rate   Voluntary unemployment

Key skills exercises

Knowledge and understanding

To answer the questions in this chapter, you need to know and understand:

- what is meant by unemployment
- the difference between the economically active and economically inactive population
- how unemployment is measured
- the difficulties of measuring unemployment
- the difference between the level of unemployment and the rate of unemployment
- the causes and types of unemployment: frictional, structural, cyclical, seasonal and technological
- the consequences of unemployment.

> **TIP**
>
> Learners often confuse the level of unemployment and the unemployment rate. An easy way to remember the difference is that the level of unemployment is the *total* number who are unemployed. The unemployment rate is expressed as a *percentage* of the entire labour force.

1 Define unemployment.
2 Describe the difference between a person who is economically active and a person who is economically inactive.

3 Describe how unemployment is usually measured.

4 Explain the difference between the level of unemployment and the rate of unemployment.

5 Describe frictional unemployment and give an example.

6 Describe structural unemployment and give an example.

7 Describe cyclical unemployment and give an example.

8 Describe seasonal unemployment and give an example.

9 Describe technological unemployment and give an example.

Analysis

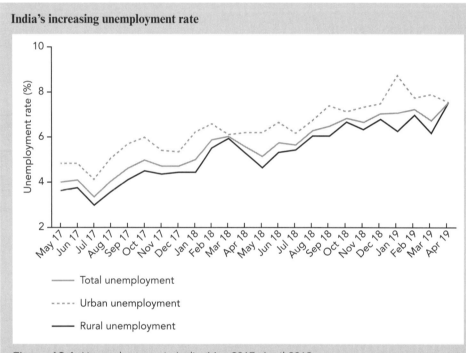

Figure 19.1: Unemployment in India, May 2017–April 2019

Source: Centre for Monitoring Indian Economy (CMIE)

India's rate of unemployment doubled between May 2017 and April 2019 when it reached 7.6%. The gap between urban and rural unemployment has closed (see Figure 19.1). The main cause for the increase in the unemployment rate is the lack of skills required for the jobs that are now available. This is worrying, given India's young population and growing evidence that unemployment rates increase with educational level. In short, India's young workforce, though well-educated, is 'technically unskilled'.

10 Explain **two** possible causes of urban unemployment in India.

19 Unemployment

> **WORKED EXAMPLE FOR Q10**
>
> One possible cause of unemployment is that some of the unemployed people lack the skills that are necessary for newly created jobs in a growing urban economy such as that of India. IT and communication skills, for example, will be essential for anyone seeking a job in a call centre or office. A second reason is that in a growing urban economy there will be frictional unemployment, with a core of workers changing jobs but with short temporary periods of unemployment in between jobs **[A]**.

11 Explain **two** possible causes of rural unemployment in India.

12 Analyse the effects of increased unemployment on India's economy.

Evaluation

13 Comment on why collecting data on unemployment in India is likely to be difficult.

14 Comment on the view that the 'main cause for the increase in unemployment (in India) is the lack of skills required for jobs that are now available'.

> **PRACTICE QUESTIONS**
>
> ### Data response question
>
> 1 **a** Using the data in Figure 19.1, describe **two** changes in the pattern of unemployment in India from May 2017 to April 2019.
>
>   **b** For each change, explain the likely reason for the change in the pattern of unemployment.
>
> ### Essay questions
>
> 1 Explain the main types of unemployment in your country (or in a country familiar to you) **and** consider which of these types accounts for the greatest percentage of those who are unemployed.
>
> 2 Explain the difference between the claimant count and the labour force survey measure of unemployment **and** consider which is likely to give the highest rate of unemployment.
>
> 3 Discuss the consequences of a high rate of unemployment for a lower middle-income economy.
>
> **Improve this answer**
>
> This is a sample answer to essay Q3.
>
> > There are various consequences of a high rate of unemployment for an economy, as well as for individuals and businesses in that economy. The consequences are particularly serious in a lower middle-income economy where new job opportunities are likely to be limited.
> >
> > Before considering these consequences, it is necessary to be clear on what is meant by a 'high unemployment rate in a lower middle-income country. It is not easy to put a percentage on this, but a figure above 8% would seem reasonable. This percentage is higher than for other richer economies **[K]**.
> >
> > The first consequence is lost output. The resources of the economy are not being used to their full potential. The economy is working within and not on its PPC. An opportunity cost is involved in terms of living standards and the quality

CONTINUED

of life being lower than if more people had been in employment. If the lost output is for export, then there will be a negative impact on the balance of trade **[A]**.

If the unemployment rate is high and has increased to this level, there is likely to be a negative effect on the government's finances. As the unemployed will have less income, receipts from indirect taxation will be reduced. A high unemployment rate is unlikely to affect revenue from direct taxation as few people pay income tax. A consequence could be less government spending on development projects but more spending on unemployment benefits **[A]**. The government may well have to borrow more if it wants to operate a budget deficit to increase the level of aggregate demand.

In a lower middle-income economy, a likely consequence is how to deal with the drift of unemployed rural, agricultural workers who move to large urban areas in search of work. Some workers may succeed, but the majority will lack the skills necessary to find employment at a time when many other people are seeking jobs **[A]**.

In some respects, businesses are less likely to be affected than individuals and the government. This is because if unemployment is high, wages may be lower than if unemployment was lower **[E]**. This keeps costs down and helps businesses to stay competitive.

The above analysis needs to be qualified in two respects. First, as stated earlier, the consequence will depend on how high the rate of unemployment is compared to previous rates **[E]**. Some unemployment can actually be good for the economy since it can reduce inflationary pressures. Second, the consequences also depend on which groups in the economy are unemployed and for how long they have been out of work. Youth unemployment and graduate unemployment are serious problems in many economies, including lower middle-income countries where the employment structure means that it is difficult for new jobs to be created for these unemployed groups **[E]**.

Your challenge

See whether you can improve this answer. This is a promising answer. The learner understands the point of the question. The answer would benefit from additional examples to support the more theoretical content. The examples could be from a country that the learner has studied. The evaluation in the final paragraph is appropriate. A better answer is given in the workbook answers – but write yours out first.

> Chapter 20
Price stability

LEARNING INTENTIONS

In this chapter you will:
- define the meaning of inflation, deflation and disinflation
- calculate the rate of inflation
- explain how changes in the price level are measured by the consumer price index
- consider the difficulties of measuring changes in the price level
- explain the difference between money values and real data
- analyse the causes and types of inflation: cost-push and demand-pull inflation
- analyse the consequences of inflation.

KEY TERMS

Annual average method   Barter   Consumer price index (CPI)   Cost-push inflation   Creeping inflation
Debtors   Deflation   Demand-pull inflation   Disinflation   Fiscal drag   Hyperinflation   Inflation
Inflationary noise   Inflation rate   Menu costs   Monetarists   Money values   Price level   Price stability
Real data   Shoe leather costs   Wage–price spiral   Year-on-year method

Key skills exercises

Knowledge and understanding and application

To answer the questions in this chapter, you need to know and understand:
- the meaning of inflation, deflation and disinflation
- how inflation is calculated
- how changes in the price level are measured
- the difference between money values and real data
- the causes of inflation
- the consequences of inflation.

> **TIP**
>
> You need to be careful when looking at data on inflation rates. Many learners think that a fall in the inflation rate means that prices have fallen. This is not true. A fall in the inflation rate means that the rate of increase in prices has fallen.

1. Define the term 'inflation'.
2. Explain what is meant by price stability.
3. Explain the difference between deflation and disinflation.
4. Describe how a consumer price index is constructed.
5. Explain how a consumer price index can be used to measure changes in the price level.
6. Explain the difference between money values and real data.
7. Explain the causes of inflation.
8. Explain the consequences of inflation.

Analysis

The causes of inflation in Pakistan

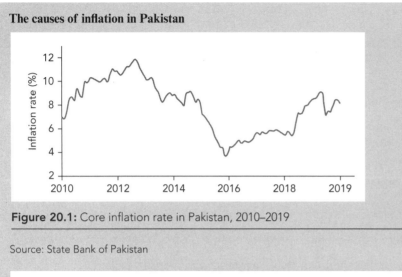

Figure 20.1: Core inflation rate in Pakistan, 2010–2019

Source: State Bank of Pakistan

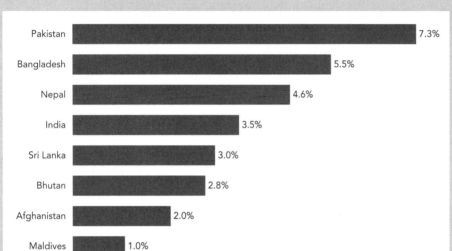

Figure 20.2: Comparative rates of inflation for Southeast Asian counties in 2019

Source: Asian Development Bank

Inflation in Pakistan is increasing again. With it comes costs, particularly for those on low incomes. Given that most people on low incomes have most of their assets in cash, their purchasing power is being eroded as everyday items increase in price. Rising inflation can affect whether families can afford healthcare or whether a child goes to school or has to work. Inflation also discourages longer-term investment by the private sector on projects that are designed to raise Pakistan's productive capacity.

There were three causes of the increase in inflation in 2018:
- growth in the money supply while aggregate supply is fixed
- rising import prices, especially for oil
- domestic supply shocks resulting from, for example, crop failure.

9 The text gives **three** causes of inflation in Pakistan. Analyse each of these causes and say how each matches the recognised causes of inflation (demand-pull, cost-push and monetary).

10 Explain **two** ways in which people on low incomes are adversely affected by a rising rate of inflation.

WORKED EXAMPLE FOR Q10

People on low incomes will find that the prices of basic food items are increasing at a faster rate than their wages. They have little or no bargaining power to increase their wages. Most poor people are unlikely to have a bank account and will be likely to keep accumulated cash savings at home. The real value of these savings will fall with the increase in inflation **[A]**.

Evaluation

11 Discuss the benefits to Pakistan's people, firms and government of a falling rate of inflation.

12 Discuss some of the problems when constructing a consumer price index for a lower middle-income country such as Pakistan.

PRACTICE QUESTIONS

Data response question

1 Using the data in Figure 20.1:
   a Describe the trend in Pakistan's core inflation rate from 2010 to 2019.
   b Identify a period of rising inflation and a period of disinflation.

Essay questions

1 Explain the main causes of inflation in a country you have studied **and** consider which of these causes is the most important at the present time.

2 Discuss the consequences of a sharp, unexpected increase in the rate of inflation in a lower middle-income country **and** whether consumers, producers or governments will be most affected by this increase.

Improve your answer

This is a sample answer to essay Q2.

> A basic definition of inflation is that it is when prices in an economy are increasing. This is a well-known phenomenon in almost all economies. Not all inflation is bad. In fact some inflation is good for an economy **[K]**. Much depends on the rate of inflation we are talking about.
>
> In my country, last year the government said that the rate of inflation was 5.2%. This was a big increase on the previous year's figure of 3.4%. The main reason for the increase was the increase in price of oil imports **[A]**. These are essential for our economy as we have no oil of our own. The figure of 5.2% is not necessarily bad but there would be concerns if it increased further.
>
> The unexpected increase in the rate of inflation has consequences for consumers, producers and the government. For consumers, the prices of everyday items will increase as the value of money decreases. This could mean that they have

CONTINUED

to spend more time comparing prices to get the best deal. Anyone with savings in a bank will also lose out as the rate of interest is invariably below the rate of inflation. Alternatively, debtors or those borrowing money are likely to gain. People who rely on government handouts are also likely to lose, as these tend not to keep pace with a change in the rate of inflation [A].

Inflation raises production costs, especially if the inflation is due to the rising cost of imported raw materials. Producers can also experience menu costs as a consequence of having to regularly alter the prices charged to customers. For businesses, inflation creates uncertainty, which tends to discourage future investment plans. They also incur what are called shoe leather costs when moving any liquid assets around from one place to another in search of the highest rate of interest [A].

Governments also experience consequences. An increase in the rate of inflation is likely to reduce a country's international competitiveness if its rate of inflation is much greater than that of its trading rivals. This can result in a fall in export expenditure by its overseas customers and a rise in import expenditure by its own people, as imported goods become rather more competitive in the domestic market [A]. Inflation can also be politically dangerous if it gets out of hand.

As can be seen above, consumers, producers and the government experience consequences of a sharp, unexpected increase in the rate of inflation. Who loses out most will really depend on the actual extent of the change and how swiftly it has come about. In the absence of more information, it is not possible to say which of the three loses out the most [E].

Your challenge

See whether you can improve this answer. The answer improves as it develops. The first paragraph is weak and inflation is poorly defined. The second paragraph is vague although the use of actual data is promising. Thereafter, the main problem is that the answer is not directed to a lower middle-income country. A better answer is given in the workbook answers – but write yours out first.

> Unit 5

Government macroeconomic intervention (AS Level)

> Chapter 21
Government macroeconomic policy objectives

LEARNING INTENTIONS

In this chapter you will:

- explain a government's macroeconomic policy objective of price stability
- explain a government's macroeconomic policy objective of low unemployment
- explain a government's macroeconomic policy objective of economic growth.

KEY TERM

Inflation target

Key skills exercises

Knowledge and understanding

To answer the questions in this chapter, you need to know and understand:

- the macroeconomic policy aims of a government.

1. What are a government's macroeconomic policy aims?
2. Describe an inflation target.
3. Explain why a government has an inflation target.
4. Explain what low unemployment means.
5. Explain why economic growth is a macroeconomic policy aim.

> **TIP**
>
> Remember that not all of the aims of macroeconomic policy can be achieved at the same time. This means that a government has to prioritise its aims. These aims can vary over time.

Analysis

Vietnam's economic progress

	2017	2018	2019	2020 (forecast)	Target
GDP growth (% year on year)	6.8	7.1	6.8	6.5	6.6–6.8
Inflation (yearly average %)	3.5	3.6	3.6	3.8	<4.0
Unemployment rate (%)	2.1	2.0	2.0	2.0	n.a

Table 21.1: Selected measures of Vietnam's economic progress, 2017–2020

Vietnam is one of the fastest growing economies in the world. In 2019, Vietnam's economic growth rate was at least 6.8%, within its annual target. An important reason for Vietnam's high growth rate has been the way the economy and its people have benefited from the growth in exports of inexpensive clothing and footwear.

Some multinational companies have moved from China into Vietnam. This has created a strong labour market with no particular unemployment problems.

Vietnam's President was very clear that macroeconomic stability had been maintained, while inflation had been kept below the target set by the National Assembly.

6   Analyse whether Vietnam's people are likely to be better off in 2020 compared to 2019.

WORKED EXAMPLE FOR Q6

GDP growth in 2020 is projected to be below that for 2019, and also below target. This will mean a smaller than expected increase in the consumption of goods and services that are available for the Vietnamese people **[A]**. The forecast for the rate of inflation in 2020 is 0.2 percentage points higher than in 2019, but below the target. Unemployment is low and stable, with continuing opportunities for new jobs to be created. It is unlikely that new jobs created by MNEs will be well-paid **[A]**.

Overall, it seems that Vietnamese people will on average be marginally better off. This is mainly due to the healthy increase in GDP growth, the benefits of which should offset the more negative aspects of increasing inflation **[E]**.

PRACTICE QUESTIONS

Essay questions

1   Explain why an increasing number of governments have set an inflation target **and** consider whether this is a realistic macroeconomic policy objective.
2   Discuss the main domestic macroeconomic policy objectives **and** say which of these should be the most important.

Improve this answer

This is a sample answer to essay Q1.

> An increasing number of governments have introduced the idea of setting a target for the rate of inflation. These countries have been diverse – low, middle and high – income countries. In some cases, the target is fixed at say 2%, in other cases it may be in the range of say 3%–5% **[K]**.
>
> Inflation is where there is a general rise in the price level in an economy. For most countries, the control of inflation is the main priority on account of the serious effects that a high level of inflation can have on consumers, firms and the economy **[K]**. Other macroeconomic policy objectives, though still relevant, tend to have a lower priority.
>
> The UK was one of the first countries to set an inflation target. It was originally set by the government, but responsibility was then transferred to a committee of economists and business leaders. The purpose of the target is for the government to adopt monetary and fiscal policies that are consistent with achieving the given target. This is difficult **[E]**. The target is unlikely to be matched each year, and is best seen as one to be met over a reasonable period of time.

CONTINUED

An important side effect of an inflation target is that it is likely to reduce or control inflationary expectations. This is especially valid with respect to cost-push inflation, which could arise from excessive demands for wage increases. The target acts as a basis for negotiations between employers and trade unions. For public sector workers, the target is likely to become the final increase in pay. An inflation target can also act as a guide to firms when projecting what future prices to charge for their products [A].

An inflation target, therefore, can be a realistic policy objective for a government. The experience of many countries has generally been a positive one, with the inflation target being central to achieving the full range of macroeconomic policy objectives [E].

Your challenge

See whether you can improve this answer. This is an effective answer. It is well structured, informative and stays focused on the point of the question. The final two paragraphs contain a reasonable amount of evaluation for an answer at this level. You could make a useful addition to the beginning of the third paragraph by including an example of an inflation target from a country you have studied and evaluate whether the target has been achieved. A better answer is given in the workbook answers – but write yours out first.

Chapter 22
Fiscal policy

LEARNING INTENTIONS

In this chapter you will:

- define the meaning of fiscal policy
- define the meaning of a government's budget
- explain the difference between a government budget deficit and a government budget surplus
- explain the meaning and significance of the national debt
- explain the difference between indirect and direct taxes
- explain the difference between progressive, regressive and proportional taxes
- explain rates of tax: marginal and average rates of taxation (mrt, art)
- analyse the reasons for taxation
- explain the difference between current and capital government spending
- analyse the reasons for government spending
- explain the difference between expansionary and contractionary fiscal policy
- discuss, using AD/AS analysis, the impact of expansionary and contractionary fiscal policy on equilibrium level of national income, the level of real output, the price level and employment.

KEY TERMS

Automatic stabilisers   Average rate of tax   Balanced budget   Budget   Budget deficit   Budget surplus   Capital government spending   Contractionary fiscal policy   Current government spending   Cyclical budget deficit   Direct taxes   Discretionary fiscal policy   Exhaustive government spending   Expansionary fiscal policy   Fiscal policy   Indirect taxes   Marginal rate of tax   National debt   Non-exhaustive government spending   Progressive tax   Proportional tax   Regressive tax   Sin taxes   Specific taxes   Structural budget deficit   Tax avoidance   Tax base   Tax evasion

Key skills exercises

Knowledge and understanding

To answer the questions in this chapter, you need to know and understand:

- what fiscal policy means
- what is included in a government's budget
- what the national debt means
- the difference between indirect and direct taxes
- the difference between progressive, regressive and proportional taxes
- why governments impose taxes
- the difference between current government spending and capital government spending
- the difference between an expansionary fiscal policy and a contractionary fiscal policy
- the effects of expansionary and contractionary fiscal policy on the equilibrium national income, the level of real output, the price level and employment.

1 Describe the scope of fiscal policy.
2 Describe the meaning of a government's budget.
3 What is the national debt?
4 With the help of examples, explain the difference between indirect and direct taxes.
5 Explain the difference between progressive, regressive and proportional taxes.
6 Describe the difference between current government spending and capital government spending.
7 Explain the difference between an expansionary fiscal policy and a contractionary fiscal policy.

> **TIP**
> An error that many learners make is to confuse fiscal policy and monetary policy. The best way to avoid any confusion is to keep reminding yourself that fiscal policy is about taxation and government spending.

Analysis

Malaysia's resilient economy

Malaysia is an upper middle-income country. The country's economy is one of the strongest, most diversified and fastest growing in Southeast Asia. Malaysia has moved from an economy dependent on rubber and palm oil production to one that produces lots of petroleum and natural gas, alongside its substantial manufacturing and service sectors.

Malaysia has used an expansionary fiscal policy to promote economic growth, create employment opportunities and improve the distribution of income while seeking to strike a balance between these objectives.

In August 2019, a meeting of economists concluded that Malaysia's economy was facing uncertainty due to growing restrictions on international trade. The economists believed that, despite Malaysia's high debt level, if the economy was badly hit in the future, there would still be an opportunity to pursue further expansionary fiscal policy measures. Strong GDP growth highlighted Malaysia's resilience to the challenging global environment.

Economic growth	4.9%
Unemployment rate	3.3%
Inflation rate	3.5%
Government debt	50.7% GDP
Gini coefficient	0.43 (2018); 0.46 (2009)
Exports	998 billion ringgit[1] (2018)
Imports	878 billion ringgit (2018)
Government spending	260 billion ringgit (2018)
Government revenue	227 billion ringgit (2018)

Note: [1]The ringgit is Malaysia's currency

Table 22.1: Key statistics for Malaysia's economy, 2019 and 2018

8 Explain why Malaysia's government might want to implement an expansionary fiscal policy.
9 Explain why the Malaysian government might want to increase government debt.
10 Analyse the likely effects of increased government spending on Malaysia's economy.

22 Fiscal policy

Evaluation

11 Consider whether Malaysia's fiscal policy is meeting its stated aim.

WORKED EXAMPLE FOR Q11

The stated aim of Malaysia's fiscal policy is to promote economic growth, create employment opportunities and improve income distribution. Considering the data for 2019 and 2018, there is clear evidence that these three objectives of fiscal policy are being met **[E]**. Economic growth is at a level associated with an emerging economy. Unemployment is low. The decrease in the Gini coefficient indicates that there is a more equal income distribution in 2018 compared to nine years earlier **[E]**. This assessment, though, is based on only one year's data. Data for other recent years and forecast data would be useful in confirming this assessment **[E]**.

12 Comment on the extent to which Malaysia's economy is likely to be resilient to the challenging global environment.

PRACTICE QUESTIONS

Data response question

1 Using the data in Table 22.1:
  a State whether Malaysia's budget was in deficit or in surplus in 2018. Justify your answer.
  b State whether Malaysia's balance of trade was in deficit or in surplus in 2018. Justify your answer.

Essay questions

1 A government decides to double its expenditure on its country's infrastructure.

With the help of aggregate demand and supply analysis, discuss whether this will be beneficial for its economy.

2 Explain why a government may need a contractionary fiscal policy **and** consider why such a policy should only be for a short period of time.

Improve this answer

This is a sample answer to essay Q1.

> Infrastructure is one of the types of government spending. It covers roads, railways, housing, airports for example. If a government decides to double its infrastructure spending, this will mean a big boost for the economy **[K]**. Aggregate demand will also double. The effect can be shown on a diagram.
>
>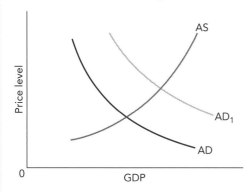

CONTINUED

> Aggregate demand increases due to the increase in G. This is shown by the shift of AD, with GDP also increasing. The result will be that more jobs are created in order to construct the new roads, houses and so on. These jobs will be among suppliers, as well as in firms who actually do the construction **[A]**. It is going to be beneficial for the economy.
>
> Where this increased expenditure is not going to be beneficial is if it creates demand-pull inflation. If so, it will reduce the benefits from the increased government spending and affect many people and businesses in the community **[A]**.

Your challenge

See whether you can improve this answer. The answer is weak in all respects and it is also short. There are various errors. Aggregate demand will not double due to leakages from the circular flow of income. The diagram is incomplete and not referred to in a positive way in the answer. There is no evaluation as to whether the effects will be beneficial. A better answer is given in the workbook answers – but write yours out first.

> Chapter 23

Monetary policy

LEARNING INTENTIONS

In this chapter you will:

- define the meaning of monetary policy
- explain the main tools of monetary policy, including interest rates, the money supply, credit regulations
- explain the difference between expansionary and contractionary monetary policy
- discuss, using AD/AS analysis, the impact of expansionary and contractionary monetary policy on equilibrium level of national income, the real level of output, the price level and employment.

KEY TERMS

Central bank   Commercial banks   Credit regulations   Interest rates   Monetary policy   Money supply

Key skills exercises

Knowledge and understanding

To answer the questions in this chapter, you need to know and understand:

- what monetary policy means
- the main tools of monetary policy: interest rates, the money supply and credit regulations
- the difference between expansionary and contractionary monetary policy
- the effects of expansionary and contractionary monetary policy on equilibrium national income, the level of real output, the price level and employment.

1. Describe the scope of monetary policy.
2. Explain the meaning of an interest rate.
3. Give a simple definition of the money supply.
4. Describe the meaning of credit regulations.
5. Describe the role of a central bank in monetary policy.
6. Explain the difference between an expansionary and a contractionary monetary policy.

> **TIP**
>
> Be clear what is meant by monetary policy. Many learners confuse monetary policy with fiscal policy. An obvious way to avoid this confusion is to keep reminding yourself that monetary policy is all about monetary measures, such as the *money* supply and the interest rate, which is what you get for *money* you might have in a bank.

Analysis

Conducting monetary policy the Fed's way

The US Federal Reserve Board, the US central bank, is responsible for the USA's monetary policy. It is mandated by the US congress to manage monetary policy subject to two objectives. These are to promote maximum (or full) employment and stable prices, with a target of 2% inflation over the period shown in Figure 23.1.

Decisions on monetary policy are taken by the Federal Open Market Committee. Most notably, this body decides on whether to raise or lower the interest rate. Lowering the interest rate, known as the federal funds rate, is seen as representing an easing of monetary policy. Raising the interest rate is a tightening.

Figure 23.1 shows the changes in the federal funds rate from 2014 to late 2019

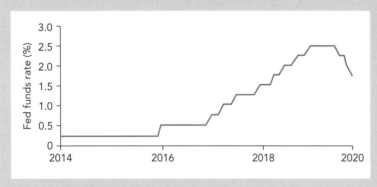

Figure 23.1: US federal funds rate, 2014–2019

Source: US Federal Reserve

7   Explain how a 'lowering of the interest rate is seen as representing an easing of monetary policy. Raising the rate is tightening'.

8   Analyse how controlling the federal funds rate allows the US central bank to promote the government's two macroeconomic objectives.

Evaluation

9   Comment on why monetary policy in the USA may not always work as suggested by economic theory.

PRACTICE QUESTIONS

Data response question

1   Using the data in Figure 23.1:
    a   Describe the changes in the Fed's Fund Rate from 2014 to 2019.
    b   State a time period when the Fed was undertaking an expansionary monetary policy **and** give a possible reason for this policy.
    c   State a time period when the Fed was undertaking a contractionary monetary policy **and** give a possible reason for this policy.

23 Monetary policy

CONTINUED

> **WORKED EXAMPLE FOR Q1**
>
> a The Fed's rate was stable at 0.25% up to the end of 2016. It then increased in a series of regular steps peaking at 2.5% at the start of 2019. It then fell quickly to 1.75% **[K]**.
>
> b During 2019. To offset fears of rising unemployment and recession **[A]**.
>
> c From late 2016 to the beginning of 2019. To control inflation to its 2% target **[A]**.

Essay questions

1 Explain how monetary policy could be used to counteract a period of deflation **and** consider whether this policy is likely to be successful.

2 Discuss whether monetary policy is the best way for a government of a middle-income country to correct inflation.

3 Discuss how an increase in the interest rate is likely to affect aggregate demand and supply **and** discuss why the effects may not always be certain.

Improve your answer

This is a sample answer to essay Q3.

> The interest rate is the price or cost of borrowing money. It is also the reward or benefit for those people who are able to save and hold their savings in financial institutions. Using interest rates to control the level of aggregate demand in the economy is the main way in which monetary policy works in practice **[K]**.
>
> An increase in the interest rate occurs when it has been determined that a contractionary or deflationary monetary policy should be adopted. This would be done if the monetary authorities were concerned that the rate of inflation was too high and having detrimental effects on the economy and on the foreign exchange rate **[A]**.
>
> A more or less immediate effect of the rise in interest rates is that consumers are likely to save more and spend less, especially if they are borrowing money to fund consumption. There is an opportunity cost involved **[A]**. The rise in interest rates will also affect business firms who find that the increased cost of borrowing now makes their investment plans far less attractive. So investment falters and aggregate demand decreases. Firms are also influenced by falling consumer demand and are likely to be less confident about their future **[A]**.
>
> Increased interest rates encourage 'hot money' to flow into an economy as overseas investors can get a better rate of return through transferring their investments from somewhere that is paying less interest. The likely consequence is an appreciation of the domestic foreign exchange rate **[A]**. This is not good news, since the price of domestic exports will increase. The higher exchange rate will encourage consumers to buy more goods from abroad. This will only serve to fuel inflation if there are intermediate goods that are used in the manufacturing industry. So the net of exports and imports is likely to fall **[A]**.
>
> The effects of an increase in interest rates may not always be straightforward. Consumers may continue to spend, especially on 'big ticket' items, if they expect a further increase in interest rates to be imminent. Similarly, firms may continue to invest if they feel confident about future market opportunities **[E]**. The impact on exports and imports will very much depend upon their price elasticities of demand **[E]**.

Your challenge

See whether you can improve this answer. The content of the answer is fine, although it is not written in an analytical style. An AD/AS diagram would enhance the answer's quality. The final paragraph includes a little evaluation, which could be developed to focus more on the point of the question, why the effects may not always be certain. A better answer is given in the workbook answers – but write yours out first.

Chapter 24
Supply-side policy

LEARNING INTENTIONS

In this chapter you will:

- define the meaning of supply-side policy in terms of its effects on LRAS curves
- explain the objectives of supply-side policy (to increase productivity and productive capacity)
- analyse the tools of supply-side policy, including training, infrastructure development and support for technological improvement
- discuss, using AD/AS analysis, the impact of supply-side policy on the equilibrium national income and the level of real output, the price level and employment.

KEY TERMS

Infrastructure   Privatisation   Supply-side policy

Key skills exercises
Knowledge and understanding

To answer the questions in this chapter, you need to know and understand:

- what a supply-side policy means
- how a supply-side policy affects the LRAS curve in an economy
- the objectives of supply-side policy tools
- typical examples of supply-side policy tools
- the effects of supply-side policy on equilibrium national income and the level of real output, the price level and employment.

1 Describe the scope of a supply-side policy.
2 Describe how a supply-side policy affects the LRAS curve in an economy.

WORKED EXAMPLE FOR Q2

A supply-side policy leads to a shift to the right of the LRAS curve. This shift will lead to an increase in real GDP **[K]**.

3 Explain the objectives of a supply-side policy.
4 Describe **four** typical supply-side policy tools.

Analysis

Foreign workers in Singapore

Singapore is a high-income country. Its economic progress since independence in 1965 has been remarkable. Where Singapore is unique is that its growing prosperity has been

> **TIP**
>
> You will find it useful to know of actual, up-to-date supply-side policy tools that are in place in your economy or in another economy you have studied. You can use these examples to improve the quality of what might otherwise be an abstract discussion.

> **TIP**
>
> It will help you to remember that supply side-policy tools always seek to increase aggregate supply. It would be pointless for governments to do otherwise.

24 Supply-side policy

through promoting free trade, welcoming foreign businesses and capital, and through the efforts of foreign workers. Figure 24.1 shows Singapore's total population by residency status from 2015 to 2019.

Figure 24.1: The composition of Singapore's population, 2015–19

Source: Singapore Department of Statistics

Singapore's migrant workers come mainly from Malaysia, China, India, Bangladesh and the Philippines. Those who are skilled have the possibility to stay in Singapore. The majority, though, are low-skilled and may find themselves out of work when Singapore's economy falters. Even so, without both groups of workers, Singapore's economy would not be where it is today.

5 Explain why attracting foreign workers in Singapore is a supply-side policy.

6 Explain how Singapore's foreign workforce is likely to change when there is a recession in the global economy.

Evaluation

7 Discuss how changes in the number of migrant workers affects real output, the price level and employment in Singapore.

8 Discuss the benefits and costs to Singapore's economy of the growing numbers of foreign migrant workers.

PRACTICE QUESTIONS

Data response question

1 Using the data in Figure 24.1:
   a Describe the changing composition of Singapore's population from 2015 to 2019.
   b Explain how the composition of Singapore's population is likely to change if there is recession in Singapore's economy.

CONTINUED

Essay questions

1. With the help of examples, consider how supply-side policies are primarily microeconomic policies aimed at making markets more efficient.
2. Explain what may cause an increase in the long-run aggregate supply in an economy **and** discuss why this increase is not always beneficial.

Improve this answer

This is a sample answer to essay Q2.

Aggregate supply is defined as the total supply in an economy. Supply-side policies are designed to increase aggregate supply by improving the efficiency of markets. This will lead to an increase in the productive capacity of the economy and so shift the LRAS curve to the right **[K]**. This is shown in the diagram below.

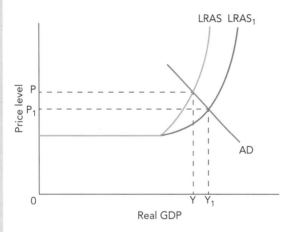

There are many types of supply-side policy. One that is strongly promoted by many countries including my own, Pakistan, is to increase the skill and educational level of the population **[A]**. This will not happen overnight, but can take a few years before having any impact on productivity and international competitiveness **[E]**.

Another policy that is being carried out in my country is privatisation of certain essential services, such as electricity and water. The privatisation, in part, of railways is also likely to happen **[A]**. As things stand, these services, which are essential for our economy, are inefficient and resources are being wasted. Privatisation should make these services more efficient, more market-focused in pricing and provide much needed new investment, something that was not happening under public ownership **[E]**.

These are just two examples of supply-side policies that are being applied by my government. Referring back to the diagram, if successful and in time, the policies will result in the aggregate supply curve shifting from LRAS to $LRAS_1$. Real output or economic growth increases and inflationary pressure is reduced as the price level falls from P to P_1. Overall, this must be beneficial **[E]**.

Your challenge

See whether you can improve this answer. This is a good answer. The final paragraph could be more explicit on why an increase in AS may not be beneficial. A minor criticism is that the examples could be more explicit and provide actual names of policies, firms and so on. Your challenge is to extend the two examples with one or two others from a country you have studied, for example a new paragraph could make reference to Pakistan's policy on both privatisation and education. A better answer is given in the workbook answers – but write yours out first.

> Unit 6

International economic issues (AS Level)

> Chapter 25

The reasons for international trade

LEARNING INTENTIONS

In this chapter you will:

- explain the difference between absolute and comparative advantage
- explain the benefits of specialisation and free trade (trade liberalisation), including the trading possibility curve
- explain how the terms of trade are measured
- analyse the causes of change and impact of changes in the terms of trade
- discuss the limitations of the theories of absolute and comparative advantage.

KEY TERMS

Absolute advantage   Comparative advantage   Economies of scale   Exports   Factor endowment
Free trade   Imports   Opportunity cost ratio   Trading possibility curve   Terms of trade

Key skills exercises

Knowledge and understanding

To answer the questions in this chapter, you need to know and understand:

- the principle of absolute advantage
- the principle of comparative advantage
- what free trade means and why free trade can be beneficial to all economies
- what is measured by the terms of trade
- reasons for a change in the terms of trade for an economy and the impact of the change
- limitations of the principles of absolute and comparative advantage.

1. Describe the principle of absolute advantage.
2. Describe the principle of comparative advantage.
3. Describe the meaning of free trade.
4. Define the terms of trade.
5. State how the terms of trade are measured.

> **TIP**
>
> Learners often struggle to understand the meaning of the terms of trade. A common mistake is to think that the terms of trade are the same as the balance of trade or something to do with an agreement when firms or a country trade with each other. The terms of trade are quite simply the relationship between export *prices* and import *prices*.

25 The reasons for international trade

Analysis

The benefits and costs of the Comprehensive and Progressive Agreement for Trans-Pacific Partnership (CPTPP)

At the end of 2018, 11 countries went ahead with the CPTPP, a radical free trade agreement between a group of countries, mainly Asian, along the Pacific rim. The early enforcers were Japan, Singapore, Australia, New Zealand, Canada and Mexico. Other members who have since ratified the agreement are Brunei, Chile, Malaysia, Peru and Vietnam.

CPTPP members are a powerful force in global trade, with 14% of world GDP. It is significant that most are in Asia, the fastest growing region in the world and with a proven commitment to globalisation. It is also significant that the UK could become a member in the future.

The benefits of the CPTPP are to create more jobs and generate economic growth in the economies of its members. Exports of vehicles, machinery and plastics are free of any restrictions, as are agricultural products such as dairy, beef and poultry. This has been a huge boost to farmers in Canada, Australia and New Zealand.

The CPTPP though is not without costs. Its free trade principles will lead to cheaper goods from low-wage countries such as Vietnam and Mexico flooding into high-income members. This will lead to unemployment in manufacturing in high-income countries, and was the main reason why the USA pulled out of an earlier Trans-Pacific Partnership agreement.

6   How might you determine whether a member of the CPTPP has an absolute or comparative advantage in the production of a particular product?

WORKED EXAMPLE FOR Q6

A simple way is to look at the value or volume of a product that is being traded. Where a country's exports are greater than its imports for the same product, it is *likely* that the country has an absolute or comparative advantage [A].

7   Analyse how the CPTPP encourages members to specialise in the production of certain goods and services.

8   Analyse why the CPTPP has led to increased concerns about Vietnamese goods entering the USA.

9   Proton is a large vehicle manufacturer based in Malaysia. Analyse the likely opportunities and threats to the company as a result of Malaysia's membership of the CTPP.

Evaluation

10 Discuss the likely benefits to members if the UK joins the CPTPP.

PRACTICE QUESTIONS

Multiple-choice question

1   The terms of trade index for Indonesia in October 2019 was 105.9. In March 2020, the terms of trade index was 102.1. Which of these is a correct description of this change?

	Change in terms of trade	By how much
A	improved	3.6%
B	improved	3.8%
C	deteriorated	3.6%
D	deteriorated	3.8%

Essay questions

1   Explain the benefits of free trade as suggested by the principle of comparative advantage **and** consider whether these benefits can be identified in the real world.
2   Discuss the effects of a change in the domestic price level and an economy's exchange rate on the terms of trade.

Improve this answer

This is a sample answer to essay Q2.

> As the name suggests, the terms of trade is the basis on which two countries agree to trade. It covers things such as the price for goods traded, the exchange rate, terms of delivery, payment requirements and so on. These terms must be agreed before any transaction occurs.
>
> If the domestic price level changes, then this will affect the price of goods being exported. Any increase in the price could lead to a fall in demand from countries buying exports. This would then reduce aggregate demand and could lead to loss of jobs in businesses that produce goods for export. It may also have a negative effect on the balance of payments of a country. On the other hand, if the domestic price level falls, this could mean that more exports are sold, as they are now more price competitive compared to exports from trading rivals **[K]**. The reverse could occur – an increase in demand, more jobs and a bigger credit in the balance of payments.
>
> Whether a country is successful in its trade also depends on the exchange rate. International trade uses US dollars to price goods. The exchange rate of any currency such as the rupee against the US dollar varies, often on a daily basis. This is why a rate of exchange is included in the terms of trade and is agreed before any business transaction take place.
>
> If a currency loses some of its value, then its exports become more expensive and its imports become cheaper. This is bad news for the economy, as it leads to a fall in aggregate demand and less credits in the country's balance of payments. When a currency appreciates against the US dollar, its exports become cheaper and more attractive to buyers. Goods imported from other countries now cost more and so consumers will buy less of them. So, to conclude, a change in the domestic price level and an economy's exchange rate have an important impact.

Your challenge

See if you can improve this answer. This is a weak answer in all respects. The definition of terms of trade in the first paragraph is wrong. This makes it very difficult to answer the point of the question. The second and third paragraphs are therefore very general, although they do show some very basic knowledge. The third paragraph lacks clarity and contains wrong statements. The last paragraph contains many conceptual errors. There is no discussion, as required by the question. A better answer is given in the workbook answers – but write yours out first.

Chapter 26
Protectionism

LEARNING INTENTIONS

In this chapter you will:
- define the meaning of protectionism as it relates to international trade
- explain the different tools of protection: tariffs, import quotas, export subsidies, embargoes and excessive administrative burdens ('red tape')
- analyse the impact of the different tools of protection
- discuss arguments for and against protectionism.

KEY TERMS

Current account   Dumping   Embargo   Exchange control   Infant industries   Monopoly
Protectionism   Quota   Tariff   Voluntary export restraint

Key skills exercises

Knowledge and understanding

To answer the questions in this chapter, you need to know and understand:
- what is meant by protectionism
- the different tools of protection and how they work
- the impact of the different tools of protection
- arguments for and against protectionism.

1. Define the meaning of protectionism in the context of international trade.
2. Describe the meaning of a tariff and give an example.
3. Explain how a tariff works.
4. Describe the meaning of a quota and give an example.
5. Explain how a quota works.
6. State the purpose of exchange control.
7. State the purpose of an embargo.
8. State the purpose of voluntary export restraint.
9. Describe the term 'infant industries'.
10. Describe the meaning of dumping and give an example.

Analysis

The USA lifts threat of tariffs on Brazilian metals

In a surprise move, the US government backed down from its threat to impose tariffs on Brazil's exports of steel and aluminium. The reason appears in part economic – US steel manufacturers require semi-finished Brazilian steel. It was also political as the USA seeks to develop stronger links with this emerging economic powerhouse. Exports of these metals from elsewhere are subject to tariffs of 25% (steel) and 10% (aluminium).

The US government had previously criticised Brazil for unfair trading practices. These included deliberately weakening the real (Brazil's currency) against the US dollar and hurting American farmers by selling increasing quantities of agricultural goods, especially soybeans, to China.

11 Analyse the impact on the US economy of a tariff on imports of steel and aluminium products.

12 Explain the likely reasons why the US government has put a higher tariff on steel products compared to the tariff on aluminium products.

WORKED EXAMPLE FOR Q12

The most likely reason is that the USA needs imports of aluminium products more than it needs imports of steel products. Also, US steel producers could be less efficient than aluminium producers and so need greater protection to stay in the market. There could also be a greater need to protect jobs in the steel industry [A].

13 Analyse how a deliberate weakening of the real (Brazil's currency) is a form of protection.

Evaluation

14 Discuss whether the USA is justified in imposing protectionist measures on trade with an emerging economy such as Brazil.

PRACTICE QUESTIONS

Multiple-choice question

1 In which of these situations will imposing a tariff on imported food be most effective?

   A   Where the price elasticity of demand is inelastic.

   B   Where the price elasticity of demand is elastic.

   C   Where the income elasticity of demand is positive.

   D   Where the cross elasticity of demand is negative.

Essay questions

1 Explain the difference between a tariff and a quota **and** consider which is best used by a high-income country.

2 Discuss whether the case for protectionism in international trade can ever be justified.

CONTINUED

Improve this answer

This is a sample answer to essay Q1.

A tariff is a tax that is levied by a government on imported goods. It can be specific in the form of a fixed amount per unit imported or it can be ad valorem as a percentage of the price. The point about a tariff is that it pushes up the price of the product, making it more expensive in the importing country. Its other purpose is to steer domestic consumers away from an imported good to the same or similar product made by firms in the domestic market **[K]**. A typical example of this is the 10% tariff levied by the European Union on vehicles that are produced elsewhere or the 12% tariff on most imported clothing.

A quota is different. It is a physical limit set by a government on particular imported goods. The idea behind it is by restricting supply, the price of the imported goods will increase **[K]**. Depending on the price elasticity of demand, the seller of the imported product could receive more revenue. A quota can often take the form of a licence which sets out how many goods or what value of goods can be imported. Examples of quotas are the restrictions that India imposes on the import of pulses and grains from a wide range of countries.

Tariffs and quotas have the same objective, to limit imported goods and to protect domestic producers. Both involve interfering with market forces through taxing supply and restricting supply in the market. A tariff can raise revenue for a government. A tariff will also increase the price of imported goods as will a quota. With a tariff, though, the consumption of the imported product may not decrease if it is price inelastic. With a quota, consumption can be expected to decrease **[A]**.

Your challenge

This is an effective answer. It covers the main subject content in a logical sequence and there are no particular errors. The style is more analytical than descriptive. Your challenge is to write a final paragraph containing some appropriate evaluation. A better version of the final paragraph is given in the workbook answers – but write yours out first.

Chapter 27

Current account of the balance of payments

LEARNING INTENTIONS

In this chapter you will:

- explain the components of the current account of the balance of payments
- calculate the balance of trade in goods, in services and in goods and services and the overall current account balance
- analyse the causes of disequilibrium in the current account of the balance of payments
- discuss the consequences of disequilibrium in the current account of the balance of payments for the domestic and external economy.

KEY TERMS

Balance   Balance of payments account   Capital account   Current account deficit   Current account surplus   Dividend payments   Exchange rate   Financial account   Imbalance   Surplus

Key skills exercises

Knowledge and understanding

To answer the questions in this chapter, you need to know and understand:

- the purpose of the balance of payments
- the components of the balance of payments account
- the components of the current account of the balance of payments
- the meaning of balance and imbalances in the current account of the balance of payments
- the meaning of the balance of trade in goods and services
- the causes of imbalances in the current account of the balance of payments
- the consequences of imbalances in the current account of the balance of payments.

1. What is recorded in the balance of payments?
2. State the **four** standard ways in which the balance of payments accounts of a country are presented.
3. Describe the **four** parts of the current account of the balance of payments.
4. Explain what is meant by the balance of trade in goods and services and how it is calculated.
5. Explain what is meant by the current account balance and how it is calculated.
6. Explain the difference between balance and imbalances in the current account of the balance of payments.

27 Current account of the balance of payments

Analysis

China's changing trade surplus

For many years, China has sold more to the USA than the USA has sold to China (see Figure 27.1).

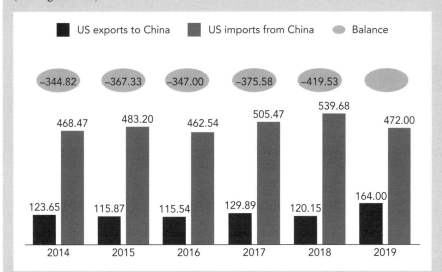

Figure 27.1: US trade balance with China, 2014–2019 (in $, billions)

Source: United States Census Bureau

This has led to the USA applying three rounds of tariffs since the beginning of 2018. These tariffs covered aerospace, IT, metals, chemicals, food products and most other goods.

In October 2019, a partial trade agreement was reached to forego further tariff escalation by the USA in exchange for China agreeing to resume the purchase of US food products. This move provided some relief to the global economy, as well as to the economies of China and the USA. Figure 27.2 shows the year on year percentage change in China's total exports and imports from January 2018 to October 2019.

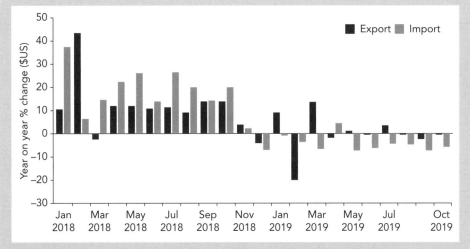

Figure 27.2: China: export and import trends, January 2018–October 2019

Source: General Administration of Customs of the People's Republic of China

7 Analyse the likely causes of imbalances in the current account of the balance of payments of the US economy.

8 Analyse the possible consequences for the US economy of imbalances in the current account of its balance of payments.

Evaluation

9 Comment upon the implications for the global economy of the USA's deficits on the current account of its balance of payments.

> ### WORKED EXAMPLE FOR Q9
>
> The USA's deficits mean that the world's largest economy has to borrow an increasing amount of funds to finance these deficits, or to release some of its foreign currency reserves [A]. This is not particularly good news and could lead to a financial crisis like that of 2008 [E]. An alternative would be for the federal government to cut back on aggregate demand to reduce the demand for imports [A]. This is difficult to implement, given the USA's federal structure. It would not go down well in economies such as China, Vietnam, South Korea and Japan that source many of the USA's imports [E].

PRACTICE QUESTIONS

Data response questions

1 Using the data in Figure 27.1, calculate the USA's trade deficit with China in 2019.

2 Using the data in Figure 27.2, compare the year on year percentage changes in China's imports and exports in 2018 with the changes up to October 2019.

3 Explain what additional information you are likely to need to get a full record of the USA's deficits on the current account of the balance of payments?

Essay questions

1 Consider whether a persistent surplus in the current account of the balance of payments is good for an economy.

2 Explain why many low-income countries have imbalances in the current account of the balance of payments **and** consider the most likely reason for these imbalances.

Improve this answer

This is a sample answer to essay Q2.

> Imbalances in the current account of the balance of payments occurs when there are persistent deficits occurring over a period of time [K]. There are many reasons for this. These will now be explained in the context of a low-income country.
>
> Most low-income countries have a comparative advantage in producing agricultural goods, although some are more fortunate and can produce certain manufactured goods, for example, trainers in Vietnam or garments in Bangladesh. Historically, the terms of trade have moved against most agricultural exports. This means that a country has to continuously produce more foodstuffs in order to retain the same value of export sales. Low-income countries producing manufactured goods can also suffer if developed economies like the USA or the EU member states impose tariffs on imported clothing and footwear. Low-income countries are also adversely affected by subsidies paid to farmers in high-income countries. The EU has been heavily criticised for such actions [A].

27 Current account of the balance of payments

CONTINUED

A second reason could be where a low-income country experiences economic growth. In turn, this is likely to increase the need for imported raw materials and capital from other countries, particularly middle- and high-income countries. The bill for imports will increase, and it may also result in more resources being allocated to domestic production rather than exports. All in all, this leads to imbalances in the current account of the balance of payments **[A]**. It may not be a bad thing in the short term as consumers will experience an increase in the quantity and quality of imported products **[E]**.

A third reason is one that is outside the control of the government of a low-income country. With respect to exports, the low-income country is dependent upon the demand from trading partners. If their economies are in a downturn, or some external shock affects their economic well-being, there is likely to be a loss of exports for the low-income country **[A]**.

It is difficult to say which is the most likely reason, as all apply. The most likely one seems to be the loss of comparative advantage due to a sustained reliance on certain types of agricultural and manufactured goods **[E]**.

Your challenge

See whether you can improve this answer. This answer contains three valid reasons why a country might have imbalances in the current account of the balance of payments. The reasons are relevant to a low-income country, which is good. One omission is that there is no reference to changes in the exchange rate and how these changes can lead to disequilibrium. Your challenge is to write one additional paragraph. A better answer is given in the workbook answers – but write yours out first.

> Chapter 28
Exchange rates

> **LEARNING INTENTIONS**
>
> In this chapter you will:
>
> - define the meaning of an exchange rate
> - explain how a floating exchange rate is determined
> - explain the difference between depreciation and appreciation of a floating exchange rate
> - analyse the causes of changes in a floating exchange rate
> - discuss, using AD/AS analysis, the impact of exchange rate changes on the domestic economy's equilibrium national income and the level of real output, the price level and employment.

> **KEY TERMS**
>
> Appreciation   Depreciation   Exchange rate   Floating exchange rate   Hot money flows

Key skills exercises

Knowledge and understanding

To answer the questions in this chapter, you need to know and understand:

- the meaning of an exchange rate
- how a floating exchange rate is determined
- the difference between depreciation and appreciation of a floating exchange rate
- why a floating exchange rate changes
- the impact of exchange rate changes on the domestic economy's equilibrium level of national income and the level of real output, the price level and employment.

> **TIP**
>
> An exchange rate is concerned with the *external* value of a country's currency, usually against the US dollar. A common error is to confuse an exchange rate with the price level, which affects the *internal* value of a country's currency.

1. State the meaning of an exchange rate and give an example.
2. Why is an exchange rate usually expressed in terms of US dollars?
3. Describe the meaning of a floating exchange rate.
4. Explain the difference between a depreciation and an appreciation of a floating exchange rate.
5. Describe the meaning of a hot money flow.

Analysis

Japanese yen to US dollar exchange rate

Figure 28.1 shows the exchange rate of the Japanese yen against the US dollar from 2010 to 2019.

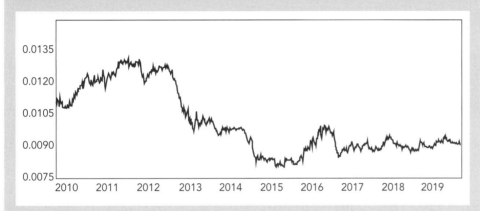

Figure 28.1: Japanese yen–US dollar exchange rate, 2010–2019

Source: www.xe.com

6 Analyse the causes of a change in a floating exchange rate such as the Japanese yen.

7 Analyse whether a depreciation or an appreciation of the US dollar against the Yen is likely to lead to an increase in the number of US visitors to Japan.

WORKED EXAMPLE FOR Q7

An appreciation of the US dollar against the yen means that American visitors to Japan will get more yen for every dollar they spend. This makes Japanese hotel prices and visits to tourist attractions relatively cheaper than when the yen was stronger **[A]**. Depending on other factors such as the price elasticity of demand for visits to Japan, there is likely to be an increase in the number of US visitors to Japan.

A depreciation of the dollar against the yen will have the reverse effect **[A]**.

Evaluation

8 Using the data in Figure 28.1, consider some of the problems of the floating exchange rate for Japanese car exporters when trading with the USA.

PRACTICE QUESTIONS

Data response questions

1 Using the data in Figure 28.1:
   a State a period when the yen has appreciated against the US dollar.
   b State a period when the yen has depreciated against the US dollar.

CONTINUED

2   Describe **two** reasons why the demand for US dollars may increase in Japan.

3   Describe **two** reasons why the supply of US dollars may increase in Japan.

Essay questions

1   Explain how a depreciation of the exchange rate can cause cost-push and demand-pull inflation **and** consider which is likely to be most damaging to the economy.

2   Discuss whether an appreciation of the exchange rate produces net benefits for an economy.

Improve this answer

This is a sample answer to essay Q1.

> A depreciation of the exchange rate occurs when a currency loses value compared to a foreign currency, usually the US dollar. A typical example is our Malaysian ringgit. Today, there are about 4 ringgits to a dollar – a year ago there were 4.2 **[K]**.
>
> The depreciation is not good news for the Malaysian people. It means that the price of imports from countries such as Vietnam and Australia fall, encouraging us to buy more clothing and meat products from them. This will be inflationary as the cost of living will increase as there may be shortages in the future.
>
> The fall in value of the ringgit also affects the price of our exports to trading partners such as Indonesia and Singapore. Export prices will increase, and it is quite likely that this will then lead to demand-pull inflation in those countries. It is also likely to result in an increase in unemployment in Malaysia.
>
> A depreciation of a currency therefore can have inflationary effects on an economy. Where the inflation is caused by cost-push factors, then it will be most damaging to an economy.

Your challenge

See whether you can improve this answer. This is a poor answer, full of errors and misconceptions. The first paragraph is a promising start – the reference to a local currency (and later to trading partners) shows that the learner is aware of the context of the question. The last three paragraphs lack detail and are full of fundamental errors. An AD/AS diagram could be used to support the text in an improved answer. A better answer (excluding the first paragraph which does not need changing) is given in the workbook answers – but write yours out first.

Chapter 29
Policies to correct imbalances in the current account of the balance of payments

> **LEARNING INTENTIONS**
>
> In this chapter you will:
> - explain the government policy objective of stability of the current account
> - analyse the effect of fiscal, monetary, supply-side and protectionist policies on the current account.

Key skills exercises

Knowledge and understanding

To answer the questions in this chapter, you need to know and understand:

- the meaning of stability in the context of the current account of the balance of payments
- how fiscal, monetary, supply-side and protectionist policies can affect the current account of the balance of payments.

1. Explain the meaning of stability in the current account of the balance of payments.
2. Explain the meaning of imbalances in the current account of the balance of payments.
3. Explain how fiscal policies can correct imbalances in the current account of the balance of payments.
4. Explain how monetary policies can correct imbalances in the current account of the balance of payments.
5. Explain how supply-side policies can correct imbalances in the current account of the balance of payments.
6. Explain how protectionist measures can correct imbalances in the current account of the balance of payments.

> **TIP**
>
> A common error that some learners make is to think that the current account of the balance of payments is the same as the balance of payments. The current account is important, but it only includes trade in goods and services, primary and secondary income. The balance of payments covers other items as well, making it a complete record of all transactions between a country and all other countries. Be careful to make it clear what you are referring to.

Analysis

Pakistan's current account turnaround?

In October 2019, Pakistan recorded its first monthly surplus on the current account of the balance of payments in over four years. A small deficit followed in November, largely due to a fall in the amount of workers' remittances.

Figure 29.1 shows a simplified representation of Pakistan's quarterly current account for July–September in 2018 and 2019.

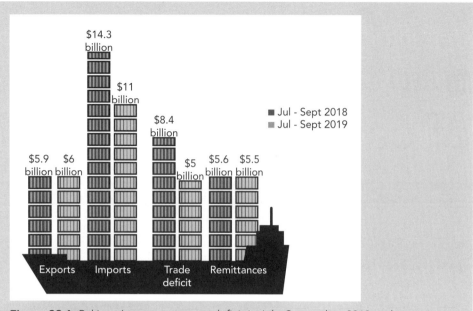

Figure 29.1: Pakistan's current account deficit in July–September 2018 and July–September 2019 (in $)

Source: Pakistan Defence

Government policy has been to concentrate on reducing the current account deficit in order to reduce foreign debt. The policy has been successful – the deficit fell by 70% between November 2018 and November 2019. However, this success has been at the cost of a massive cut in imports and the lowest rate of growth for nine years.

7 Analyse how cutting imports is likely to have affected consumers in Pakistan.

WORKED EXAMPLE FOR Q7

Cutting imports will reduce the quantity and value of goods purchased from other countries. There is also likely to be a reduction in the quality of goods available to Pakistan's population. Some imported goods will be replaced by goods that are produced domestically or cheaper goods from elsewhere, both of which may be of lower quality. It is also likely that the range of goods available to consumers will be less. Non-essential luxury products are likely to have been subject to an import ban [A].

8 Analyse how cutting imports has led to a reduction in Pakistan's rate of economic growth.

Evaluation

9 Using the data in Figure 29.1, comment on the importance of remittances for the stability of the current account of Pakistan's balance of payments.

10 Discuss what policies, other than cutting imports, the Pakistan government could use to reduce its current account deficit.

TIP

Economic data is often presented in the media in the form of a picture. Figure 29.1 is a typical example. Learners will find this form of representation useful in highlighting the main features in data.

29 Policies to correct imbalances in the current account of the balance of payments

PRACTICE QUESTIONS

Data response questions

1. Using the data in Figure 29.1, describe the main features of Pakistan's current account of the balance of payments
2. The data in Figure 29.1 has been simplified for publication in a newspaper. Say why this has been done.
3. Consider how the data in Figure 29.1 is not consistent with the text.

Essay questions

1. Discuss whether an appreciation of the exchange rate will always lead to a reduction in a current account surplus on the balance of payments.
2. Discuss how supply-side policies can be used to reduce a deficit on the current account of the balance of payments.

Improve this answer

This is a sample answer to essay Q2.

A deficit occurs on the current account of the balance of payments when the receipts from goods and services traded internationally are less than the equivalent expenditure [K]. More simply, when the value of imported goods and services is greater than those exported.

Such a deficit is not of major concern if it occurs occasionally. It is serious though when the deficit is recorded over a number of years, since it can lead to the erosion of foreign currency reserves and the accumulation of foreign debt. Repaying such debt is a common problem facing many low- and middle-income countries that depend heavily on imports of oil and raw materials but trade mainly in agricultural goods for which prices have been declining [A].

Supply-side policies should be used where a country has had persistent deficits in its current account balance. These policies, if effective, aim to improve competitiveness by shifting the aggregate supply curve to the right as shown in the diagram below.

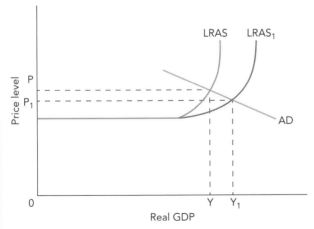

The shift of LRAS represents an increase in the quantity or quality of the factors of production. This increases an economy's productive capacity, with output increasing from Y to Y_1. Assuming no change in aggregate demand, there will be a reduction in inflationary pressures on the economy as the price level falls from P to P_1. This will be a very positive way in which to improve a country's competitiveness [A].

CONTINUED

This is the theory. The problem in practice is how an economy can achieve this shift of AS. It is particularly difficult for low-income countries. There are various supply-side policies that can be used, and these include improved education and training, encouraging more investment, better incentives to get more people to join the labour force and reform of trade unions. Most of these policies tend to be long-term and not short-term **[A]**.

This last point is particularly relevant for education and training. If labour in an economy is more skilled, the quality of human capital improves. Relevant policies include changing the school leaving age, grants to go to university, more apprenticeship opportunities and encouraging more women to join the labour force. These supply side policies should improve the quality and quantity of human resources. If applied, they ought to develop the exports of a country and to cut back on imports, so reducing the current account deficit **[E]**.

Your challenge

See whether you can improve this answer. The first paragraph consists of a sound introduction to supply-side policies. This is followed by a general account of how supply-side policies work. This is a weakness, given the wording of the question. Consequently, the answer lacks focus on the point of the question, which is how supply-side policies can reduce a deficit on the current account of the balance of payments. There is a hint of evaluation in the last paragraph. For this type of essay question, more explicit evaluation is required. A better answer is given in the workbook answers – but write yours out first.

Unit 7
The price system and the microeconomy (A Level)

Chapter 30
Utility

LEARNING INTENTIONS

In this chapter you will:

- define the meaning of total utility and marginal utility
- calculate total utility and marginal utility
- explain diminishing marginal utility
- explain the equi-marginal principle
- derive an individual demand curve
- evaluate the limitations of marginal utility and its assumptions of rational behaviour.

KEY TERMS

Equi-marginal principle   Law of diminishing marginal utility   Marginal utility   Total utility   Utility

Key skills exercises

Knowledge and understanding

To answer the questions in this chapter, you need to know and understand:

- what is meant by utility
- the meaning and calculation of total utility and marginal utility
- the law of diminishing marginal utility
- the significance of the equi-marginal principle
- how to derive an individual demand curve
- the limitations and assumptions of utility theory.

> **TIP**
>
> Utility can be measured, but it is important to remember that the benefit from consumption that a person gets varies from one good to another. It also varies from one person to another person.

1. Define the term 'utility'.
2. Describe what is meant by total utility and how it is calculated.
3. Describe what is meant by marginal utility and how it is calculated.
4. Explain the law of diminishing marginal utility.
5. Explain the equi-marginal principle.

Analysis

> **Precautionary buying and utility**
>
> There have been many instances where panic buying has followed a natural disaster, such as a hurricane or a tsunami. People's reactions are understandable as future supplies will be seriously disrupted.
>
> Consumers' reaction to the COVID-19 pandemic is not seen as panic buying. Economists and other experts have called this 'precautionary buying'. What happened is that consumers have rushed to stock up on necessities, particularly cleaning products, toilet paper, cooking oil, pasta, rice and flour. Retailers have often been forced to limit sales of such essential items.
>
> Precautionary buying makes consumers feel better. Consumers have the satisfaction of having a stock of critical supplies, even if their behaviour has taken away supplies from others. The difference between precautionary buying and panic buying is that the interruption of supplies is only short term. Within a few weeks, supplies will return to normal and many consumers will be left with much of the stock that they rushed to buy as a precaution.

6 Analyse how the demand curve for a product is derived.

7 Explain how the demand curve for a necessity product is likely to be affected by precautionary buying.

WORKED EXAMPLE FOR Q7

The demand curve for a necessity product will shift to the right assuming no change in price. This means that demand for the product has increased but at the same price **[A]**. It is likely that retailers may increase prices or limit the quantity demanded in order to dampen demand **[A]**.

Evaluation

8 Discuss the extent to which consumers are acting rationally when precautionary buying necessities such as flour, rice and cooking oil.

PRACTICE QUESTIONS

Multiple-choice question

1 A consumer gets 10 units of satisfaction when consuming a pizza that costs $2 and 2 units of satisfaction when consuming an ice cream. Assuming the consumer is rational, what is the price of the ice cream?

- **A** $0.20
- **B** $0.40
- **C** $2
- **D** $4

CONTINUED

Essay questions

1 Assess the extent to which marginal utility can be used to provide an accurate representation of a consumer's demand curve for a product.
2 Assess whether the equi-marginal principle has any relevance in determining how consumer equilibrium is achieved.

Improve this answer

This is a sample answer to essay Q2.

> The consumption of a good or service produces utility, which enables consumers to satisfy their wants. The term utility is described as the satisfaction from consuming a particular good or service. Economic theory assumes that consumers are rational and that they will always strive to maximise the total utility from what they consume. A consumer is said to be in consumer equilibrium where this is so **[K]**.
>
> When a consumer is in equilibrium, it is not possible to switch expenditure from one good to another in order to increase total utility. Assuming a given level of income and prices that do not vary with consumption, consumer equilibrium applies when the following is true:
>
> $$\frac{MU_x}{P_x} = \frac{MU_y}{P_y} = \frac{MU_z}{P_z} = \frac{MU_n}{P_n}$$
>
> This is known as the equi-marginal principle. It states that consumer equilibrium applies when the ratio of the marginal utility to price for all products consumed is equal. When this is reached, an individual is unable to re-allocate income to increase utility any further **[A]**.
>
> It follows from the equation that if the price of any good changes, this will affect the marginal utility or satisfaction that is gained from consumption of the product. In principle, this can have a ripple effect on the consumption of all other products that are consumed **[A]**.
>
> This principle is based on the assumption that consumers have a limited income and are consistently seeking to maximise their utility.

Your challenge

See whether you can improve this answer. The answer contains some sound economic analysis of the equi-marginal principle, but it lacks evaluation, as required by the command word in the question ('Assess'). The evaluation should stress the assumptions that underpin the theory, and whether consumers really do behave in a rational way in making consumption decisions. The answer is short for an essay question of this type and two concluding paragraphs of evaluation will help. A better answer is given in the workbook answers – but write yours out first.

Chapter 31
Indifference curves and budget lines

LEARNING INTENTIONS

In this chapter you will:

- define the meaning of an indifference curve and a budget line
- explain the causes of a shift in the budget line
- analyse the income, substitution and price effects for normal, inferior and Giffen goods
- evaluate the limitations of the model of indifference curves.

KEY TERMS

Budget line   Giffen good   Income effect   Indifference curve   Marginal rate of substitution   Substitution effect

Key skills exercises

Knowledge and understanding

To answer the questions in this chapter, you need to know and understand:

- what an indifference curve represents
- the nature of a budget line
- what is meant by the income effect of a price change
- what is meant by the substitution effect of a price change
- the meaning of a Giffen good.

> **TIP**
>
> Learners often have difficulty drawing diagrams to show the income and substitution effects of a price change. A diagram is not always necessary. You can explain the income and substitution effects in words.

1. Describe the characteristics of an indifference curve.
2. State why indifference curves never cross.
3. Describe what is meant by the marginal rate of substitution.
4. Explain the income effect of a price change.
5. Explain the substitution effect of a price change.
6. Define a Giffen good.
7. You will see that Figure 31.1 (see next page) is incomplete. It is designed to show what happens when there is a rise in the price of good X, a normal good. Copy the diagram and insert a full set of labels.

Analysis

Indifference curves: do we really make choices this way?

When it comes to buying things we want, economics is sometimes clear on what restricts our choices. An obvious variable is our income, particularly disposable income. A second factor is prices. In both cases, economics is really quite good at modelling our choices. But what about our likes and dislikes? These are also very important.

Our preferences are very important in deciding how we should spend our money. After all, if you hate something, there is no way you will buy it. With most things, there are many options available to us. Consider, for example, food. Do you eat chicken, fish, pizza, or are you vegetarian or vegan? If we only take two of these, there are many combinations that give us the same level of utility or satisfaction. There are also many combinations where we are indifferent. This is where the indifference curve model fits in and why economists use diagrams like the one in Figure 31.1 to analyse our choices.

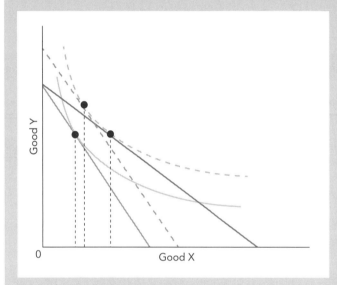

Figure 31.1: Indifference curves

8 Redraw Figure 31.1 to analyse the income and substitution effects of a rise in price of good X.

Evaluation

9 Discuss the extent to which consumers behave in the rational way that is assumed in indifference curve analysis.

WORKED EXAMPLE FOR Q9

A rational consumer is one who will always respond in the logical way put forward by economic theory, in this case, the indifference curve model. Indifference curves do not cross, and it is assumed that a consumer will always seek to reach the highest possible level of satisfaction. **[A]**. Consumers may not be rational, for example, if they put a maximum limit on one or more of their purchases or if they decide not to purchase a particular good as it has no utility for them **[E]**.

31 Indifference curves and budget lines

PRACTICE QUESTIONS

Multiple-choice question

1   Which of these statements is correct when the price of a Giffen good decreases?
    A   The positive income effect is greater than the substitution effect.
    B   The positive income effect is less than the substitution effect.
    C   The substitution effect is less than the negative income effect.
    D   The substitution effect is greater than the negative income effect.

Essay questions

1   'Indifference curves and budget lines can be used to show why consumers will normally buy more of a good at a lower price than when the price of a good increases'.
    Assess why this statement may not always be true.
2   With the help of indifference curve analysis, evaluate the difference between the income and substitution effects of a fall in the price of normal goods and inferior goods.

Improve this answer

This is a sample answer to essay Q2.

> In the case of normal goods, it is true that consumers will normally buy more of a good when its price decreases. This means that the consumer's real income has increased. The overall increase in quantity demanded can be divided into an income effect and a substitution effect **[K]**. In this case both effects are positive. When the price of a good increases, consumers will tend to buy less of this good, as their real income has decreased. Here the income effect is negative, but with a positive substitution effect. The result is a decrease in consumption of both goods **[A]**.
>
> The above sequence of effects may not always be true. This is because of two extreme cases: these are the cases of inferior goods and Giffen goods.
>
> An inferior good is one that when real income increases consumers will tend to substitute better quality goods for inferior goods. A consumer, for example, may spend more money on fresh meat and vegetables and less on rice or bread. Another example would be to spend less on meals from street stalls and more on meals in a local restaurant **[K]**.
>
> The overall change in demand can be divided into an income effect and a substitution effect. An increase in real income can come about if the price of an inferior good decreases. The fall in price will lead to consumers buying more of this product. This is a substitution effect, with more being consumed. The income effect will be negative, a consequence of consumers now substituting more expensive products for the inferior good. These effects are shown in the diagram. The substitution effect is the movement along the indifference curve from E_1 to E_2 and is (as always) positive. The income effect is the change from E_2 to E_3 and is negative resulting in less of good X being consumed. The income effect is negative but not as strong as the substitution effect **[A]**.

CONTINUED

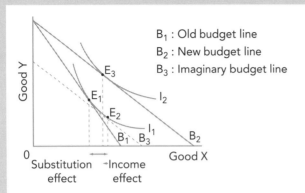

B$_1$: Old budget line
B$_2$: New budget line
B$_3$: Imaginary budget line

To conclude, in addition to the inferior goods case, the big assumption made with indifference curve analysis is that consumers always act in a logical, rational manner. This is not always the case. Some consumers, for example, may not want to change their consumption of the two goods, irrespective of changes in their price. The theory is also simplified. In the real world, consumers have to choose between many goods, making it difficult to choose between different combinations **[E]**.

Your challenge

See whether you can improve this answer. The answer has some good points but could be improved by making a closer link between the diagram and the content in the fourth paragraph. The first paragraph could be shortened to explain the meaning of a normal good and an inferior good. The explanation of the income and substitution effects is covered in later paragraphs. The case of a Giffen good should be considered in more detail. A better answer is given in the workbook answers – but write yours out first.

Chapter 32
Efficiency and market failure

LEARNING INTENTIONS

In this chapter you will:
- define the meaning of productive efficiency and allocative efficiency
- explain the conditions needed for productive efficiency and allocative efficiency
- explain Pareto optimality
- define the meaning of dynamic efficiency
- define the meaning of market failure
- explain the reasons for market failure.

KEY TERMS

Allocative efficiency   Dynamic efficiency   Economic efficiency   Pareto optimality   Productive efficiency

Key skills exercises

Knowledge and understanding

To answer the questions in this chapter, you need to know and understand:
- the meaning of economic efficiency
- the meaning of productive efficiency and allocative efficiency
- conditions needed for productive efficiency
- conditions needed for allocative efficiency
- the meaning of Pareto optimality
- the meaning of dynamic efficiency
- conditions for dynamic efficiency
- reasons for market failure
- consequences of market failure.

> **TIP**
>
> When discussing productive efficiency, a common error is to not make clear the difference between production and productivity. Production refers to the total that is produced. Productivity is a measure of how much is produced per worker or per hour worked.

1. Define the term 'economic efficiency'.
2. Explain the meaning of productive efficiency.
3. Explain the meaning of allocative efficiency.
4. Explain the meaning of Pareto optimality.
5. Explain the meaning of dynamic efficiency.
6. Explain the reasons for market failure.

Analysis

International comparisons of labour productivity

Productivity is how much output is produced for a given input such as an hour of work. In Figure 32.1, GDP per hour is used as a measure of labour productivity. This measure shows how efficiently labour is used with the other factors of production. Variations in labour productivity have macroeconomic implications – the more efficient an economy, the more goods and services that can be produced. In turn, this leads to a higher long-term growth rate for the economy.

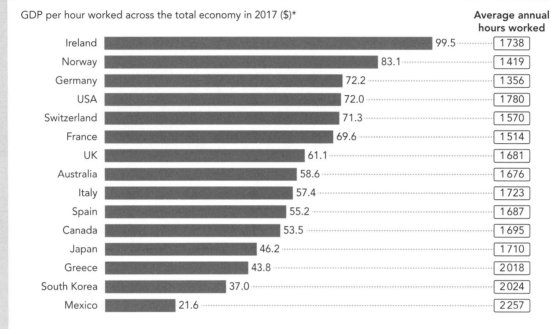

* Selected countries (current prices and PPPs)

Note: Purchasing power parity uses an exchange rate based on the amount of each currency needed to purchase the same basket of goods and services in each country.

Figure 32.1: Labour productivity in selected countries, 2017

Source: OECD

7 Analyse the conditions needed for productive efficiency.

8 Analyse the conditions for allocative efficiency.

9 Analyse the conditions for dynamic efficiency.

10 Analyse the consequences of market failure.

11 Analyse the differences in labour productivity for the countries shown in Figure 32.1.

Evaluation

12 Evaluate the extent to which variations in average annual hours worked might explain the differences in labour productivity for the countries shown in Figure 32.1.

32 Efficiency and market failure

> **WORKED EXAMPLE FOR Q12**
>
> There is a relationship between productivity and the annual hours worked for countries at the top and bottom end of the ranked data. For example, Norway and Germany are the second and third ranked in terms of labour productivity. They have the two lowest average annual hours worked. Ireland does not match this relationship. The three lowest countries in terms of productivity are Greece, South Korea and Mexico. These countries have the three highest average annual hours worked **[A]**.
>
> Labour productivity is a complex topic and is affected by many other factors as well as hours worked. These factors include the rate of increase of capital investment, technological change and wage rates **[E]**.

PRACTICE QUESTIONS

Multiple-choice question

1. The table below shows the number of units of labour and capital that are required to produce a given quantity of output. A unit of labour costs $100 and a unit of capital costs $400.

   Which of the combinations of labour and capital is productively efficient?

	Output	Labour input	Capital input
A	10	4	1
B	20	7	2
C	30	10	3
D	40	15	4

Essay questions

1. Evaluate the extent to which the privatisation of a manufacturing industry is likely to lead to greater economic efficiency.
2. Assess why the market mechanism increasingly fails to produce the most efficient allocation of resources.

Improve this answer

This is a sample answer to essay Q2.

> The market mechanism is where resources are allocated by the twin forces of demand and supply and without government intervention. When working as it should, the market mechanism will produce the most efficient allocation of resources **[K]**.
>
> Economic efficiency consists of allocative and productive efficiency. A good way of explaining efficiency is the production possibility curve. Allocative efficiency can be represented by any point on the PPC, as both goods are being produced using all of the resources available. Productive efficiency is where firms are producing the goods that are required. It is where price equals marginal cost.

CONTINUED

The market mechanism does not always lead to the most efficient allocation of resources. This is the reason why a government has to provide public goods and merit goods. If the government were not to do this, poorer groups in the economy would not experience the quality of life they would like [A]. Another example of market failure is where there is a monopoly seller in the market. The seller produced a lower output and sells the product at a higher price than would be the case in a market that is free [A].

Your challenge

See whether you can improve this answer. This is a weak answer, well below what is required. The second paragraph is of no value since the learner confuses productive efficiency and allocative efficiency. The third paragraph contains two relevant examples, but there is no attempt to relate these examples to productive and allocative efficiency. A better answer is given in the workbook answers – but write yours out first.

Chapter 33
Private costs and benefits, externalities and social costs and benefits

LEARNING INTENTIONS

In this chapter you will:
- define the meaning of a negative externality and a positive externality
- define the meaning of private costs and benefits, external costs and benefits and social costs and benefits
- calculate private costs and benefits, external costs and benefits and social costs and benefits
- analyse negative and positive externalities of production and consumption
- analyse the deadweight welfare losses arising from negative and positive externalities
- explain asymmetric information and moral hazard
- evaluate the use of costs and benefits in analysing decisions.

KEY TERMS

Adverse selection   Asymmetric information   Benefit:cost ratio   Cost–benefit analysis   Deadweight welfare loss
External benefit (EB)   External costs (EC)   Externality   Moral hazard   Negative externality   Positive externality
Private benefit (PB)   Private costs (PC)   Shadow price   Social benefit (SB)   Social costs (SC)   Third party

Key skills exercises

Knowledge and understanding

To answer the questions in this chapter, you need to know and understand:
- what is meant by an externality
- the various types of costs and benefits arising from an action
- the difference between negative externalities and positive externalities
- the difference between production externalities and consumption externalities
- what is meant by asymmetric information and moral hazard
- the nature and use of cost–benefit analysis.

1 Define the term 'negative externality'.
2 Define the term 'positive externality'.
3 State what is meant by a third party.
4 Explain the difference between private, external and social costs.

5 Explain the difference between private, external and social benefits.
6 Explain the difference between production and consumption externalities.
7 Describe what is meant by asymmetric information.
8 Describe what is meant by moral hazard.
9 Explain the purpose of a cost–benefit analysis.

Analysis

China's new drive to cut down on 'white pollution'

China may be the world's largest producer and user of single-use plastic, but it is also the most advanced country when tackling the growing problem of plastic waste.

Globally, the world's oceans are full of plastic waste. Every year, millions of birds, mammals and fish die from eating or getting caught up in plastic waste. In China, as elsewhere, so-called 'white pollution' caused by discarded plastic bags, bottles and other plastic products has contaminated soil and rivers, before making its way into the sea. There is also growing evidence that white pollution can affect public health, particularly through the consumption of fish.

The Chinese government has strongly promoted the development of biodegradable plastic bags and containers. It has now gone further by announcing a ban on non-degradable plastic bags in major cities by 2021. The ban will then be extended to all cities and towns by 2022. The ban will also apply to other single-use plastics such as take-away food containers and drinking straws.

10 Analyse the negative externalities associated with the global increase in plastic pollution.
11 Analyse the positive externalities associated with the increased production and use of biodegradable plastics in China.

WORKED EXAMPLE FOR Q11

The positive externalities are the side effects that provide unexpected benefits to third parties. The extensive use of biodegradable plastics will be to the overall benefit of the community, especially those who live close to rivers or in coastal areas. These benefits will also be to people using beaches that are no longer polluted with white plastic waste. There will also be less of a health risk to people who drink water or eat fish that are caught in polluted waters [A].

TIP

Whether an externality is due to a production action or a consumption action is not always clear. To clarify which it is, put yourself in the position of the third party who has been affected by the action. This should help you to decide.

Evaluation

12 Comment on the costs and benefits involved in banning the use of single-use plastics in Chinese towns and cities.

33 Private costs and benefits, externalities and social costs and benefits

PRACTICE QUESTIONS

Multiple-choice question

1 A person discards a single-use plastic bag near a river and the bag gets caught up in the net of a local fisherman. Which of these terms best describes this externality?

   A negative production externality
   B negative consumption externality
   C positive production externality
   D positive consumption externality

Essay questions

1 Evaluate the extent to which cost–benefit analysis should be the only means for evaluating whether a publicly funded project should proceed.
2 Assess the view that there will always be a deadweight welfare loss when there is a negative production externality in the market.

Improve this answer

This is a sample answer to essay Q2.

> A negative production externality occurs when there is a misallocation of resources in the production process. This results in detrimental spill over effects on third parties who have nothing at all to do with the production action **[K]**. A typical example is where a chemical factory emits toxic waste into the local environment. This pollutes the air and can cause distress and discomfort to those people who live close by.
>
> A situation like that above can be shown in a diagram.
>
>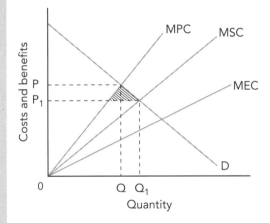
>
> The deadweight welfare loss is the loss of welfare due to the market failure of there being overproduction. From society's point of view, a better allocation of resources occurs when the factory produces less chemicals and the price paid by customers of the factory is higher **[K]**.

CONTINUED

In conclusion, where a negative production externality exists in a market, there will be most likely a misallocation of resources, which results in a welfare loss **[A]**. The reason for this is that the marginal private cost of an activity is not equal to the marginal social cost since there are external costs that have to be taken into account. These external costs are borne by third parties as a result of the factory emitting toxic fumes **[A]**.

The only time that there will be no deadweight welfare loss is when there are no external costs. This will be where marginal private cost is equal to marginal social cost **[E]**.

Your challenge

See whether you can improve this answer. This answer contains some sound economic knowledge and analysis. The point of the question is understood and made very clear in the final paragraph. The main weakness is that the diagram is wrong. MPC and MSC are the wrong way round. The deadweight welfare loss is not shown correctly and there is no real attempt to analyse the diagram in the body of the answer. It is essential when using a diagram in your answer that it is correctly drawn and then specifically referred to in your answer. Your challenge is to add three new paragraphs, including a diagram, to the end of the learner's answer. A better answer is given in the workbook answers – but write yours out first.

> Chapter 34

Types of cost, revenue and profit, short-run and long-run production

LEARNING INTENTIONS

In this chapter you will:

- explain the short-run production function, including: fixed and variable factors of production; total product, average product and marginal product; the law of diminishing returns (law of variable proportions)
- calculate total product, average product and marginal product
- explain the short-run cost function, including: fixed costs and variable costs; total, average and marginal costs; the shape of short-run average cost and marginal cost curves
- calculate fixed costs and variable costs, and total, average and marginal costs
- explain the long-run production function, including no fixed factors of production and returns to scale
- explain the long-run cost function, including the shape of the long-run average cost curve and the minimum efficient scale
- analyse the relationship between economies of scale and decreasing average costs
- explain internal economies of scale and external economies of scale
- explain internal diseconomies of scale and external diseconomies of scale
- define the meaning of total, average and marginal revenue
- calculate total, average and marginal revenue
- define the meaning of normal, subnormal and supernormal profit
- calculate supernormal and subnormal profit.

KEY TERMS

Average product   Average revenue (AR)   Decreasing returns to scale   Diseconomies of scale   Economies of scale
External economies of scale   Firm   Fixed costs (FC)   Isocosts   Isoquant   Increasing returns to scale
Law of diminishing returns   Marginal product   Marginal revenue (MR)   Minimum efficient scale   Normal profit
Price maker   Price taker   Production function   Profit   Profit maximisation   Subnormal profit
Supernormal profit   Total product   Total revenue (TR)   Variable costs (VC)

Key skills exercises

Knowledge and understanding

To answer the questions in this chapter, you need to know and understand:

- the short-run and long-run production function
- the short-run and long-run cost function

- the relationship between economies of scale and decreasing average costs
- the difference between internal and external economies of scale
- the difference between internal and external diseconomies of scale
- the difference between normal, subnormal and supernormal profits.

1 State the law of diminishing returns.
2 Define the term 'fixed costs'.
3 Define the term 'variable costs'.
4 Explain the difference between increasing returns to scale and decreasing returns to scale.
5 Distinguish between internal and external economies of scale.
6 Explain the difference between normal profit, subnormal profit and supernormal profit.

Analysis

The power of Walmart

Walmart is easily the biggest retailer in the world, with an estimated turnover of over $500 000m in 2018. Walmart has 11 500 stores in 27 countries and e-commerce websites in ten countries. Walmart's slogan is 'Save money. Live Better' and indicates the importance of the firm's huge buying power. Walmart is able to benefit from cconomies of scale due to the number of stores it owns and the ways in which it manages its supply chain. Walmart, like its competitors, operates on low net profit margins, typically about 2% of turnover.

Figure 34.1 shows one way that Walmart and other large retailers can obtain economies of scale. This is known as the container principle – increasing the surface area of a truck leads to a more than proportionate increase in the volume of capacity, which leads to a reduction in the unit costs of goods carried. This reduction in unit costs is maximised when a fully loaded truck delivers goods to a single store.

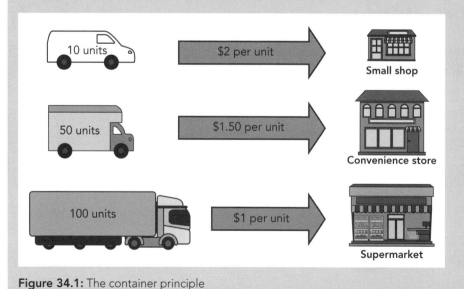

Figure 34.1: The container principle

> **TIP**
>
> Large firms benefit most from economies of scale. A common misconception is that a small firm cannot experience economies of scale. As a small business expands its operations, economies of scale will begin to occur.

7 Analyse the long-run relationship between average total costs and output.

8 Excluding the container principle, analyse **three** other types of internal economies of scale that may benefit large retailers such as Walmart.

9 Analyse how a large retailer such as Walmart might benefit from external economies of scale.

Evaluation

10 Discuss whether large retailers such as Walmart are ever likely to experience diseconomies of scale.

11 Comment on whether Walmart is earning normal or supernormal profit.

PRACTICE QUESTIONS

Data response question

1 Using the information in Figure 34.1, explain the container principle.

> **WORKED EXAMPLE FOR Q1**
>
> As the dimension of the area for carrying goods increases, there is more than proportionate increase in the capacity available for carrying goods. So, the doubling of the surface area of the truck produces a five times increase in the volume of load that can be carried. A further doubling from a capacity of 50 units also doubles the volume that can be transported. The increases in capacity lead to significant falls in unit costs **[A]**. This is a practical example of economies of scale.

Essay questions

1 Assess the view that large firms will know when they can benefit from economies of scale, but will not know when diseconomies of scale happen.

2 The cost fixity problem occurs when a firm has a high proportion of fixed costs to variable costs in the short run.

   Evaluate the likely impact of the cost fixity problem on the prices and profitability of a firm.

Improve this answer

This is a sample answer to essay Q2.

> Fixed costs are those costs that are independent of output. They are long-run costs since all costs can be varied in the long run. Variable costs, as the name suggests, vary directly with the output that is produced. The short run is the time period when at least one factor input is fixed and cannot be changed **[K]**.
>
> Fixed costs are the costs a firm has to pay to use its fixed factors of production. Examples include the rental payments a firm has to make for its premises, insurance charges, interest on bank loans and fixed charges for water and electricity. The point is that these costs do not change with the level of output or service provided. Even if the firm ceases production, it is still liable to pay its fixed costs **[K]**.

CONTINUED

Variable costs are the costs a firm has to pay for the use of its variable inputs into the production process. A typical example is labour. If a firm wants to produce more output, it will have to increase the number of workers it employs. The same is true with raw materials, the costs of which will depend on the amount of output **[K]**.

Some firms have a high proportion of fixed costs to variable costs. An example is a hotel. Once a hotel is open to customers, then variable costs are incurred. The variable costs will depend on what percentage of rooms is sold – the higher this is, the greater will be the proportion of variable costs to total costs **[A]**. Other examples of firms with a cost fixity problem are theatres, airlines, restaurants and sporting fixtures, all of which have a perishable product which cannot be transferred to another day if unsold.

A firm with this cost structure must seek to cover its variable costs in the short run. So, the price charged must at least equal the average variable costs. It will only begin to earn profits when all costs are covered. These costs will include normal profits.

Your challenge

See whether you can improve this answer. The answer is superficial and lacks focus on the point of the question. The final paragraph begins to focus on what is required, but much more depth and evaluation is needed. There should be more clarity on when fixed costs have to be paid. The answer could be enhanced with a diagram. A better answer is given in the workbook answers – but write yours out first.

> Chapter 35
Different market structures

LEARNING INTENTIONS

In this chapter you will:

- describe the market structures of perfect competition and imperfect competition (monopoly, monopolistic competition, oligopoly and natural monopoly)
- explain the characteristics of the market structures in terms of the number of buyers and sellers, product differentiation, degree of freedom of entry and availability of information
- explain barriers to entry and exit (legal, market, cost, physical)
- analyse the performance of firms in different market structures through:
  - revenues and revenue curves
  - output in the short run and in the long run
  - profits in the short run and in the long run
  - shutdown price in the short run and in the long run
  - deriving a firm's supply curve in a perfectly competitive market
  - efficiency and X-inefficiency in the short run and in the long run
  - price competition and non-price competition
  - collusion and the Prisoner's Dilemma in oligopolistic markets (including a two-player pay-off matrix)
- define the meaning of a concentration ratio
- calculate a concentration ratio
- analyse the features and implications of contestable markets.

KEY TERMS

Barrier to exit   Barriers to entry   Cartel   Collusion   Concentration ratio   Contestability   Contestable market
Deregulation   Imperfect competition   Kinked demand curve   Limit pricing   Market structure
Monopolistic competition   Monopoly   Natural monopoly   Non-price competition   Oligopoly
Perfect competition   Predatory pricing   Price competition   Price leadership   Price rigidity   Pure monopoly
Shut-down price   X-inefficiency

Key skills exercises

Knowledge and understanding

To answer the questions in this chapter, you need to know and understand:

- the meaning of market structure
- the characteristics of perfect competition, monopolistic competition, oligopoly, monopoly and natural monopoly
- what is meant by barriers to entry and exit
- the short-and long-run performance of firms in perfect competition, monopolistic competition, oligopoly, monopoly and natural monopoly

- what is meant by a concentration ratio and how to calculate it
- the features and implications of contestable markets.

1 Define the term 'market structure'.
2 Explain the characteristics of perfect competition.
3 Explain the characteristics of monopolistic competition.
4 Explain the characteristics of oligopoly.
5 Explain the characteristics of monopoly and natural monopoly.
6 Explain the purpose of barriers to entry.
7 Outline examples of barriers to entry.
8 Describe what is meant by a barrier to exit.
9 Explain the characteristics of a contestable market.
10 Define a concentration ratio and state how it is calculated.

> **TIP**
>
> When discussing or writing about a monopoly, it is good practice to make clear what sort of monopoly you are describing. In some cases this will be about a pure monopoly which has full 100% control over the market. A firm is also classed as a monopoly when it has a very large market share. It is not possible to put a figure on this as it varies from one industry to another and from one country to another.

Analysis

Mobile subscriptions in Malaysia

Malaysia has a population of around 32m. In 2018, remarkably, it had almost 43m mobile subscribers, making Malaysia one of the most mobile-saturated countries in the world.

The market for mobile subscriptions is shown in Table 35.1. This table gives the market share of the four biggest suppliers. These suppliers own their own network infrastructure. Other firms are known as Mobile Virtual Network Operators (MVNOs) since they provide their services using networks provided by other companies.

Company	2015*	2018
Maxis	29%	23%
Celcom	28%	21%
Di Gi	27%	28%
U Mobile	8%	17%
Others (incl. MVNOs)	8%	11%

*Author's estimate

Table 35.1: % market share of mobile subscribers, 2015 and 2018

Providing mobile network subscriptions is a competitive business, with firms mainly employing methods of non-price competition.

11 Explain the likely market structure of the mobile subscriptions market in Malaysia.
12 Analyse how you would expect firms to compete in the mobile subscriptions market in Malaysia.

Evaluation

13 Comment on what additional data or information you would need to be more certain of the likely market structure of the mobile subscriptions market in Malaysia.

35 Different market structures

PRACTICE QUESTIONS

Data response question

1 **a** Using the data in Table 35.1, analyse the changes in the provision of mobile subscriptions in Malaysia between 2015 and 2018.

    b Explain **two** likely reasons for the changes you have observed.

> **WORKED EXAMPLE FOR Q1**
>
> **a** The four firm concentration ratio decreased from 92% to 89%. The 3 firm concentration ratio fell from 84% in 2015 to 72% in 2018. In terms of market share, the biggest change has been recorded by U Mobile. Its market share has more than doubled to 17%. The biggest loser has been Maxis [A].
>
> **b** The indications are that the changes are due to non-price competition. For example, a company like U Mobile could be promoting a better contract deal than its competitors, or possibly offering the latest new model of device to attract consumers from competitors [A].

Essay questions

1 Assess the view that monopolies do not work in the best interests of consumers or the economy as a whole.

2 Evaluate the extent to which, when markets are more contestable, this is beneficial for consumers and firms compared to when markets are less competitive.

Improve this answer

This is a sample answer to essay Q2.

> The concept of a contestable market was developed by the US economist Baumol, who believed that the introduction of more competition into the domestic airline market would produce substantial benefits for consumers. The underlying principle of contestability is that it requires the removal of barriers to entry into an industry. Barriers such as regulations or state ownership mean that new firms are prohibited from entering a market. The US experience has proved to be an important pointer for other economies. Governments such as the UK's have used the USA's evidence to develop contestable markets in their own economies [K].
>
> The removal of barriers to entry is designed to not only allow new firms to enter an industry, but also to encourage a pool of potential entrants to be ready to enter this industry. These firms may do this if they see that supernormal profits are being earned by existing firms. It should also be stressed that there should be no sunk costs. Exit from the industry is costless [A].
>
> The ideas underpinning a contestable market are close to those of perfect competition, because there are no barriers to entry or exit. Economic efficiency is being applied, normal profits are being earned in the long run and, in principle, there is no limit to the number of firms in the market [A].

CONTINUED

It is clear that consumers should benefit when a market becomes more contestable. This would most likely be through deregulation or the privatisation of a former state-run monopoly. Costs will be reduced, which in turn will mean lower prices for consumers. Experience of when this has occurred has shown that innovation can take place. With airlines, for example, new routes and operating services from secondary airports have come about. So the greatest benefits for consumers will be in markets such as monopolistic competition, where there are low barriers to entry. In other markets, patents and other devices could hold back the market becoming more contestable **[E]**.

The benefits to firms are more difficult to assess. For those operating in a contestable market, normal profit is the norm in the long run. Any excess profits will be competed away by new entrants. A negative consequence, though, is that a contestable market lends itself to 'hit and run' entry. This is the term used when firms only enter the market for a short time while supernormal profits are being earned **[E]**.

Your challenge

See whether you can improve this answer. This is a very good answer. It is well written, authoritative and to the point of the question. The final two paragraphs contain relevant evaluation. A few more examples would enhance the answer and give more depth and development to the answer. Your challenge is to write a paragraph with examples from a country that you have studied to follow the first paragraph. A better answer is given in the workbook answers – but write yours out first.

Chapter 36
Growth and survival of firms

LEARNING INTENTIONS

In this chapter you will:

- explain reasons for the different sizes of firms
- explain the difference between internal and external growth of firms
- analyse the methods, reasons and consequences of integration (horizontal, vertical, conglomerate)
- analyse the conditions and consequences for an effective cartel
- discuss the principal–agent problem.

KEY TERMS

Conglomerate   Diversification   Economies of scope   Horizontal integration
Principal-agent problem   Vertical integration

Key skills exercises

To answer the questions in this chapter, you need to know and understand:

- reasons for the different sizes of firms
- the difference between internal and external growth of firms
- the difference between horizontal and vertical integration
- the characteristics of a conglomerate
- the conditions and consequences for an effective cartel
- the principal–agent problem.

> **TIP**
>
> It is good practice to include real-world examples based on the growth and survival of firms, especially if these are from your own country or one you have studied.

1. Describe what is meant by a conglomerate.
2. Describe what is meant by small and medium-sized enterprises (SMEs).
3. Explain what is meant by diversification.
4. Explain the difference between horizontal and vertical integration.
5. Describe how a cartel works.
6. Explain the principal–agent problem.

Analysis

Small firms in South Korea

Small and medium enterprises (SMEs) accounted for an estimated 88% of employment and 38% of South Korea's exports in 2018. In the capital Seoul, there were a staggering 823 000 SMEs. Table 36.1 shows their main areas of business.

Area of business	% of SMEs
Wholesale and retail	27
Accommodation and food service	16
Transport	12
Personal services and repairs	9
Manufacturing	7
Professional and scientific services	5
Other	24

Table 36.1: Small and medium enterprises in Seoul, 2018

SMEs have tended to be eclipsed by South Korea's conglomerates, such as Samsung Electronics, Hyundai Motors and POSCO (a huge steel maker). These flagship companies have tended to attract South Korea's young qualified workers. Very few of these workers have ended up being employed in SMEs.

A more worrying problem for SMEs is South Korea's declining population, which makes it increasingly difficult for them to fill job vacancies. The government has recognised this issue by announcing a new programme of financial assistance making it easier for SMEs to move into more promising industries. Finance is also available for SMEs to improve their facilities.

7 Analyse **two** reasons for the different sizes of firms in South Korea.

8 Analyse how companies such as Samsung and Hyundai might have diversified to achieve growth.

Evaluation

9 Comment on the extent to which the principal–agent problem affects different sizes of firms.

PRACTICE QUESTIONS

Data response question

1 Using the data in Table 36.1, explain the characteristics of SMEs in Seoul in 2018.

WORKED EXAMPLE FOR Q1

The main characteristic of SMEs is that they are labour intensive businesses. Most will have a very small number of employees. Owners may have just one or two businesses. SMEs in manufacturing may be rather larger in size. Some of these firms are likely to provide specialist services to conglomerates. The smallest firms, such as market stalls and restaurants, are likely to be family-owned and in the same ownership for many years [A].

36 Growth and survival of firms

CONTINUED

Essay questions

1. Evaluate why consumers lose out in markets where there are a small number of large firms, yet benefit in markets that have a large number of small firms.
2. Assess why it is possible for small firms to operate alongside large firms in all types of markets in all types of economy.

Improve this answer

This is a sample answer to essay Q1.

> In all types of economy, small firms tend to be the main form of business organisation. In South Korea, SMEs (defined as firms with fewer than 250 employees) provided an estimated 88% of employment in 2018. Alongside SMEs are large multinational enterprises and conglomerates **[K]**. These companies tend to be the ones that attract most attention.
>
> One of the main reasons for a difference in the size of firms is barriers to entry. In particular, a lack of capital means that it is impossible for small firms to enter an industry. An example is the telecommunications industry which in most countries has a small number of large firms. This industry is capital-intensive, restricting it to firms that have strong financial power in a competitive market **[A]**.
>
> If the market is an oligopoly, consumers may not always benefit if there is no price competition between firms. This would be especially the case if there was informal collusion between the main players **[A]**.
>
> Another example is the case of grocery markets. Owning a large supermarket requires substantial capital. For a supermarket to remain competitive, it will have to be able to take advantage of economies of scale, otherwise it will be forced to close down **[A]**. This market also has a place for small firms, such as local convenience stores where little capital is required to set up a business.
>
> Small firms are dominant in markets that are monopolistically competitive. Examples include food stalls, small hotels, restaurants, hairdressers and driving schools. As well as capital, the size of the market is a relevant factor. Markets for these services tend to be local and therefore limited in size. Because of their competitive nature, firms earn only normal profits in the long run. There is therefore less chance of consumers being exploited **[A]**.
>
> Not all small firms operate in a competitive market. Some small firms may be a monopoly. This can occur where a firm is the only producer in a local market or where a firm may be a specialist providing services for much larger firms **[A]**. Another example is where a small firm may have an advantage over a large firm in a niche market where X-inefficiency may be present.

Your challenge

See whether you can improve this answer. The answer contains some relevant content. The links to market structure are an effective way of establishing whether consumers benefit. The final paragraph should be evaluative. There are two hints at evaluation (small firms may be a monopoly; small firms may operate in a niche market) but these hints are not adequate as an evaluation. A better answer is given in the workbook answers – but write yours out first.

Chapter 37
Differing objectives and policies of firms

LEARNING INTENTIONS

In this chapter you will:

- analyse the traditional profit-maximising objective of firms
- explain other objectives of firms, including survival, profit satisficing, sales maximisation and revenue maximisation
- analyse price discrimination, including the conditions for effective price discrimination and the consequences of price discrimination
- evaluate other pricing policies, including limit pricing, predatory pricing and price leadership
- explain the relationship between price elasticity of demand and a firm's revenue for a downward sloping demand curve and a kinked demand curve.

KEY TERMS

Cross-subsidisation   Profit satisficing   Revenue maximisation   Sales maximisation

Key skills exercises

To answer the questions in this chapter, you need to know and understand:

- the meaning of profit maximisation as an objective
- other objectives of firms such as survival, profit satisficing, sales maximisation and revenue maximisation
- price discrimination and the conditions for effective price discrimination and the consequences of price discrimination
- limit pricing, predatory pricing and price leadership
- the relationship between price elasticity of demand and a firm's revenue for a downward sloping demand curve and a kinked demand curve.

1 Explain the conditions for profit maximisation.
2 Explain the meaning of survival as an objective for a firm.
3 Explain the meaning of profit satisficing.
4 Explain the meaning of sales maximisation.
5 Explain the meaning of revenue maximisation.
6 Describe what is meant by price discrimination.
7 Explain the difference between limit pricing and predatory pricing.
8 Explain the meaning of price leadership.

> **TIP**
>
> When considering the objectives of firms, the starting point should always be the objective of profit maximisation. You should then note that it is extremely difficult for firms to identify when this occurs, which is why other objectives have a greater applicability to the actual objectives of firms.

Analysis

> **Limon Chai plc**
>
> Limon Chai is a manufacturer of a popular cold tea drink. The firm is owned by a small number of investors, none of whom is involved in the day-to-day running of the company. The investors' only concern is that their investments generate an acceptable rate of return.
>
> The three senior directors of the company cannot agree the firm's strategic objective.
>
> The chief executive officer (CEO), who has just completed an online economics course, is convinced that the firm's objective should be one of profit maximisation. After all, as she tells other investors, this is what economists have promoted for many years.
>
> The marketing director is not convinced. He wants to set a target of 10% growth in revenue per annum for the next few years. To achieve this, he will need an increase in the company's marketing budget, particularly for digital marketing.
>
> The production director is concerned. She reminded her colleagues that the firm was working at almost full capacity, with machinery that had now been fully depreciated. She was also mindful that the workers were pushing for a pay increase and better working conditions. She made the point that if the company's sales were increasing, the workers would want a share of the added profits.
>
> An additional factor was that Limon Chai's main competitor had recently been sold to a US-owned multinational drinks company. The CEO believes that the board should take this into account when establishing what the company's objective should be. Her own view was that the company should reduce costs and the price of its cold tea drink.

9 Analyse the likely benefits of price discrimination for Limon Chai.

10 Analyse the relationship between price elasticity of demand and Limon Chai's revenue.

Evaluation

11 Evaluate whether profit satisficing is the best objective for Limon Chai to pursue.

PRACTICE QUESTIONS

Multiple-choice question

1 Which of these is an example of predatory pricing?

   A When a firm sells its goods at a loss.

   B When a firm buys more factors of production than it needs in order to increase costs for competitors.

   C When a firm lowers its prices to stop new firms entering a market.

   D When a firm lowers its prices to force a newly-established firm from the market.

CONTINUED

WORKED EXAMPLE FOR Q1

D.

Predatory pricing aims to force new firms out of the market. C is a definition of limit pricing – the process is the same but low prices are designed to stop new firms entering a market before they can become established. A is a more general form of pricing. B is about costs and not prices [K].

Essay questions

1. Assess whether profit maximisation is the best objective for a firm in a monopolistically competitive market.
2. Evaluate the extent to which firms in the same industry are likely to have different objectives.

Improve this answer

This is a sample answer to essay Q1.

A market is monopolistically competitive when many firms are competing with each other. Firms are price makers, but compete with each other through non-price competition. Their products are differentiated, and there is limited information available to firms in the market. There are many examples of monopolistically competitive markets such as restaurants, small hotels, driving schools, bakers and take-away food shops. These firms may be selling similar products, hence each firm has a sort of monopoly over its own products [K].

Economic theory assumes that the firm's objective is one of profit maximisation. The short-run market equilibrium is shown in the diagram.

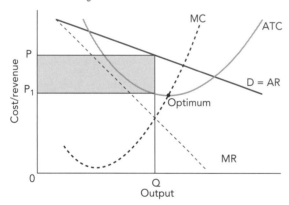

The firm is earning supernormal profit. Over time, this state of affairs will attract new firms to enter the market. The effect of this will be to shift the firm's demand curve to the left, a process that will continue until only normal profit is being earned. Normal profit is incorporated into the costs of a firm so it can be argued that from a long-term standpoint, this will be sufficient to keep a firm in the market [A].

Other objectives of a monopolistically competitive firm should also be considered. Sales maximisation involves maximising the volume of sales. This could be difficult in small firms unless there is spare capacity. Firms in monopolistic competition are inefficient since price is above average cost. This could mean that spare capacity is available to increase sales [A].

Profit maximisation would seem to be the best objective for the firm, as it will produce a steady normal level of profit in the long run.

37 Differing objectives and policies of firms

> **CONTINUED**
>
> **Your challenge**
>
> See whether you can improve this answer. The answer has only a limited focus on the question. Too much time has been spent on writing about monopolistic competition and drawing the figure. This background content should be reduced. There is a need therefore to focus more on the objectives of firms, including those not yet referred to. There is no evaluation in the answer. A better answer is given in the workbook answers – but write yours out first.

> Unit 8

Government microeconomic intervention (A Level)

> **Chapter 38**
Government policies to achieve efficient resource allocation and correct market failure

LEARNING INTENTIONS

In this chapter you will:

- explain how a range of tools can be used to correct the different forms of market failure, including specific and *ad valorem* indirect taxes, subsidies, price controls, production quotas, prohibitions and licences, regulation and deregulation, direct provision, pollution permits, property rights, nationalisation and privatisation, provision of information and behavioural insights and 'nudge' theory
- evaluate the effectiveness of the tools used to correct market failure
- define the meaning of government failure in microeconomic intervention
- explain the causes and consequences of government failure.

KEY TERMS

Government failure   Nationalisation   'Nudge' theory   Pollution permit   Production quota
Property rights   Provision of information   Regulations

Key skills exercises

Knowledge and understanding

To answer the questions in this chapter, you need to know and understand:

- government policies to correct negative and positive externalities: specific and *ad valorem* indirect taxes, subsidies, regulations, pollution permits, property rights, provision of information
- behavioural insights and 'nudge' theory
- direct provision of goods and services
- nationalisation and privatisation
- the causes and consequences of government failure in microeconomic intervention.

> **TIP**
>
> Governments provide an ever-increasing amount of information. When writing about this topic, try to think about why this is necessary and what the likely impact might be. There may well be government failure.

1. Explain the difference between a specific and an *ad valorem* indirect tax.
2. State what is meant by a regulation.
3. Explain the meaning of property rights.
4. Explain the purpose of a pollution permit.

38 Government policies to achieve efficient resource allocation and correct market failure

5 Explain why governments provide information.

6 Explain the purpose of 'nudge' theory.

7 Explain what is meant by government failure.

Analysis

The growing need for information provision

There are many ways in which governments seek to correct market failure. Providing information is a relatively recent method. It is also becoming increasingly used, especially to warn consumers of the consequences of over-consuming demerit goods. Some examples are provided in Figure 38.1.

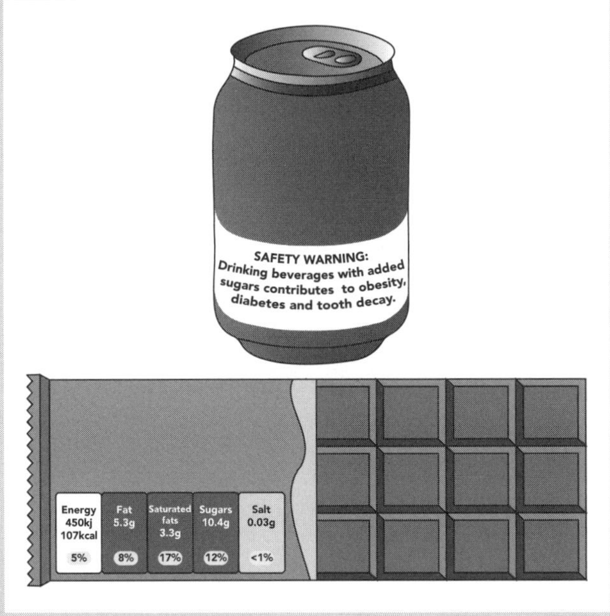

Figure 38.1: Examples of information provision on consumer goods

8 Analyse why governments directly provide goods and services.

WORKED EXAMPLE FOR Q8

Governments directly provide public goods, such as fire and rescue services, flood defences and street lighting. **[K]**. This is because it is not possible to charge for public goods. Governments also provide merit goods either free of charge or at a subsidised price. This is due to imperfect information. Families are often unaware of the benefits to themselves and the wider community and economy of providing inoculations and healthcare and some types of education **[A]**.

9 Analyse why nationalisation might correct market failure.

10 Analyse how the provision of information is expected to affect the consumption of demerit goods.

Evaluation

11 Discuss whether the provision of information is the best way of reducing consumption of sugary drinks and chocolate bars.

PRACTICE QUESTIONS

Multiple-choice question

1 Which of these situations is a case of government failure?

A When the government collects less revenue from the tax on sugar-heavy fizzy drinks than it spends on providing information on the health dangers of over-consumption of these drinks.

B When the government reduces the tax on sugar-heavy fizzy drinks and increases spending on providing information on the dangers of over-consumption of these drinks.

C When the government increases the tax on sugar-heavy fizzy drinks and increases spending on providing information on the dangers of over-consumption of these drinks.

D When the government fails to do anything about the increase in the consumption of sugar-heavy fizzy drinks among teenagers.

Essay questions

1 Evaluate the best way for a government to correct production externalities.

2 Assess why government intervention in markets to correct market failure can lead to a loss of economic welfare.

Improve this answer

This is a sample answer to essay Q2.

> There are many reasons why governments intervene in markets to correct market failure. Typical situations are where there are externalities, where there is a need for public goods and merit goods and where it is necessary to correct information failure. Intervention can take the form of indirect taxes, subsidies, property rights, regulations and other forms of indirect and direct intervention **[K]**.
>
> It is often assumed, wrongly, that all government interventions are successful in correcting market failure. Such cases are referred to as government failure, and involve a loss as against a gain in economic welfare **[A]**.
>
> One of the biggest problems being faced by governments is a lack of information, or more significantly, a lack of correct information. Without this, governments are uncertain as to what the impact of their policies might be. Instead of correcting market failure, the problems could be made worse by a government's action. An example could be in the case of pollution permits that feature in the 'cap and trade' systems that operate in some countries. The basic price of the pollution permit is critical. If the price of permits is too low, there will be little incentive for polluting firms to reduce pollution, as it will be cheaper for them to pollute than to spend capital on improving outdated pollution control technology in the company **[A]**.
>
> A second problem that governments have to tackle is that at times, their actions and policies may produce what are called unintended outcomes. A good example is in the case of an increase in the income tax rate, particularly for high earners **[A]**. Suppose the government introduces a high income tax rate of 60% for incomes earned above a particular

38 Government policies to achieve efficient resource allocation and correct market failure

CONTINUED

level. Assume also that this is the first time that such a rate has been levied. The outcome of the rise could be no more than an increase in revenue for the government. If so, this would be good. An unintended consequence, though, could be where a high income earner decides to cut back on hours worked, preferring to spend more time on leisure [A]. Another person in the same income group may decide to emigrate or move to a so-called tax haven. These events are unplanned, and not in the government's best interests.

Your challenge

See whether you can improve this answer. The answer is sound. The content and examples are competent and provide the basis for a much better answer. To achieve a higher quality answer, the learner needs to provide at least one more example and add a new concluding paragraph that clearly makes an evaluation. The 'loss of economic welfare' aspect of the question must be developed, especially in the concluding paragraph. Your challenge is to write two new final paragraphs. A better answer is given in the workbook answers – but write yours out first.

Chapter 39
Equity and redistribution of income and wealth

LEARNING INTENTIONS

In this chapter you will:

- explain the difference between equity and equality
- explain the difference between equity and efficiency
- analyse the distinction between absolute poverty and relative poverty
- describe the poverty trap
- evaluate policies towards equity and equality such as negative income tax, universal benefits and means-tested benefits and universal basic income.

KEY TERMS

Absolute poverty   Equality   Extreme poverty   Means-tested benefits   Negative income tax   Poverty trap   Relative poverty   Universal basic income   Universal benefits

Key skills exercises

Knowledge and understanding

To answer the questions in this chapter, you need to know and understand:

- the difference between equity and equality
- the definition of extreme poverty
- the meaning of absolute poverty
- the meaning of relative poverty
- why some households experience the poverty trap
- the difference between means-tested and universal benefits
- the meaning of universal basic income
- the scope for a negative income tax.

> **TIP**
>
> Be aware that most of the content of this chapter is about policies to improve the distribution of income. Sometimes you may need to discuss policies to improve the distribution of wealth as well as income. All policies have had only a modest impact in meeting their objectives.

1. Explain the difference between equity and equality.
2. How does the World Bank define extreme poverty?
3. Explain the difference between absolute poverty and relative poverty.
4. Explain the reasons why some households experience the poverty trap.
5. Explain the difference between means-tested and universal benefits.
6. Explain the meaning of universal basic income.
7. Explain how a negative income tax system works.

Analysis

South Africa: the most unequal distribution of income in the world

South Africa has the most unequal distribution of income of any country in the world. The Gini coefficient was estimated at 0.63 in 2019. In 1996 it was 0.61.

The extent of inequality is shown in Figure 39.1.

The difference between pay levels

The difference in income between the bottom and top earners in South Africa is massive. A farm worker can earn as little as R100 per day while some high level professionals can earn in excess of R3000 per day.

South African wealth distribution

10% of the population continues to earn more than 50% of the household income in the country.

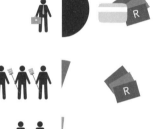

The poorest 40% of the population accounts for less than 7% of the household income.

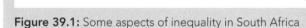

The poorest 20% accounts for less 1.5% of the income in South Africa.

Figure 39.1: Some aspects of inequality in South Africa

Wealth inequality in South Africa is even more extreme. Research by an economist at Stellenbosch University has estimated that the wealthiest 1% of the population owns 67% of all of the country's wealth. The top 10% of the population have 93% of the wealth. This means that 90% of the population own just 7% of the country's wealth.

Although annual GDP growth has been between 0.8% and 1.3% since 2014, GDP per head has been closer to nil. This leaves little scope for the government to reduce poverty. Unemployment is a key challenge. The unemployment rate was 27% in early 2019. It was even higher at 55% for youths.

A report by the Rawson Property Group recognised four ways in which the distribution of income could be improved. These are:

- increased job creation
- higher levels of education
- skills training
- low cost housing.

8 Has South Africa's distribution of income improved since 1996? Justify your answer.

9 Using the information in Figure 39.1, analyse the likely reasons for the unequal distribution of income in South Africa.

10 Explain the likely reasons why the distribution of wealth in South Africa is more unequal than the distribution of income.

CAMBRIDGE INTERNATIONAL AS & A LEVEL ECONOMICS: WORKBOOK

Evaluation

11 Evaluate which of the four policies stated in the Rawson Property Group report is likely to produce an improvement in the distribution of income in South Africa.

PRACTICE QUESTIONS

Data response question

1 Explain why the information in Figure 39.1 is inconsistent with that provided below it in the feature.

> **WORKED EXAMPLE FOR Q1**
>
> Figure 39.1 confuses income and wealth. The data in the figure is for income distribution and not wealth distribution. This is a common source of confusion [E].

Essay questions

1 Assess the extent to which the state provision of benefits seeks to achieve both equity and equality.
2 Evaluate the view that economic growth is the most effective way of combating poverty in lower middle-income countries.

Improve this answer

This is a sample answer to essay Q2.

> Poverty occurs in all economies. Poverty is a situation where a family does not have enough income to be able to experience a reasonable standard of living. By this, it is where a family has sufficient food, adequate accommodation and some access to other things such as education, healthcare and sanitation [K].
>
> Economists define poverty in various ways. The World Bank defines extreme poverty where a family is forced to exist on less than $1.90 per day. On this basis, the biggest concentrations of extreme poverty are in Sub-Saharan Africa and in South Asia. Many millions of people have moved out of this extreme form of poverty as a result of economic growth [A].
>
> Absolute poverty is different. It is not possible to put a monetary value on it as it varies from one country to another. Absolute poverty is where a household's income is too low for its members to meet even their basic needs. Inevitably, they are trapped in the vicious cycle of poverty, and are unable to benefit from economic growth [A].
>
> Relative poverty is where a household's income is compared with the average income of the country. If their income is less than half of the average, the household is said to be in relative poverty. This level of income allows basic needs to be met but access to healthcare, education and non-essential consumer goods is restricted by the low income. Economic growth is the main way in which people in this type of household are able to move out of relative poverty through becoming better off.

Your challenge

See whether you can improve this answer. The answer is short for an essay of this type. The content on the three forms of poverty is generally sound and provides the foundation for a very good answer. The main problem is that although economic growth is mentioned in three places, the link between economic growth and poverty alleviation needs to be much clearer and analysed in more depth. This should be followed by a few sentences of evaluation of the extent to which economic growth is the most effective way of combating the various forms of poverty with explicit reference to lower middle-income countries.. Your challenge is to add three concluding paragraphs. A better answer is given in the workbook answers – but write yours out first.

Chapter 40
Labour market forces and government intervention

LEARNING INTENTIONS

In this chapter you will:

- explain why the demand for labour is a derived demand
- define the meaning of marginal revenue product of labour
- calculate the marginal revenue product of labour and use marginal revenue product to derive an individual firm's demand for labour
- analyse the factors affecting demand for labour in a firm or in an occupation
- analyse the causes of shifts in the demand curve and movements along the demand curve for labour in a firm or in an occupation
- analyse the factors affecting the supply of labour in a firm or in an occupation, including wage and non-wage factors
- analyse the causes of shifts in the supply curve and movements along the supply curve for labour in a firm or in an occupation
- analyse wage determination in perfect markets, including equilibrium wage rate and employment in a labour market
- evaluate wage determination in imperfect markets, including the influence of trade unions, government and monopsony employers
- explain the determinants of wage differentials by labour market forces
- define the meaning of transfer earnings and economic rent
- evaluate the factors that affect transfer earnings and economic rent in an occupation.

KEY TERMS

| Derived demand | Economic rent | Marginal revenue product (MRP) | Minimum wage | Monopsony | Trade union |
| Transfer earnings | Wage differential |

Key skills exercises

To answer the questions in this chapter, you need to know and understand:

- why the demand for labour is a derived demand
- the meaning of the marginal revenue product of labour
- the factors affecting the demand for labour in a firm or in an occupation
- the factors affecting the supply of labour in a firm or in an occupation
- how wages are determined in perfect and in imperfect markets
- what determines wage differentials
- the difference between transfer earnings and economic rent in explaining variations in earnings in the same or different occupations.

1 Why is the demand for labour a derived demand?

2 Explain what is meant by the marginal revenue product of labour.

3 Explain the factors that affect the demand for labour in a firm or in an occupation.

4 Explain the factors that affect the supply of labour in an occupation.

5 Explain how wages are determined in a perfect market.

6 Explain the difference between transfer earnings and economic rent in an occupation.

Analysis

Is low productivity holding back Malaysia's growth?

Malaysia, one of Asia's 'Tiger economies', has experienced an average rate of real GDP growth of around 6% per year since the 1970s. Its economy has been transformed from its former heavy reliance on rubber and other agricultural products. At the present time, it has extensive automotive and electronics industries, gas and oil production and a growing service sector knowledge economy. Malaysia's government is hoping it will attain high-income status by 2024.

An OECD (Organisation for Economic Co-operation and Development) report in 2019 highlighted one potential threat to Malaysia's high-income aspiration. This threat is that labour productivity growth is weak. The report goes as far as to claim that Malaysia's economic progress is too heavily dependent on capital accumulation and not labour productivity growth. Only an estimated 8% of Malaysia's real GDP growth can be attributed to improved labour quality.

Figure 40.1 shows two measures of how Malaysia's productivity compares to that of other developing and advanced economies.

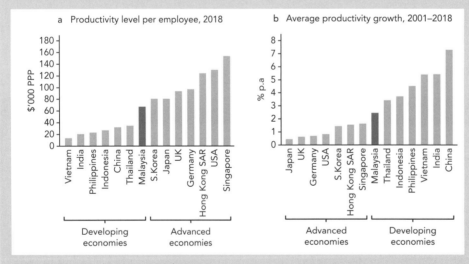

Figure 40.1: Productivity in Malaysia

Source: OECD

PPP-Purchasing power parity.

40 Labour market forces and government intervention

7   Explain the difference in the two types of data used in Figure 40.1.
8   Using the data in Figure 40.1a, analyse how Malaysia's productivity level per employee in 2018 compared with that in other developing economies and in advanced economies.
9   Explain how increased labour productivity might improve Malaysia's competitiveness.

Evaluation

10 Comment on the likely obstacles facing the Malaysian government's aspiration to be a high-income country by 2024.

> **TIP**
>
> When you refer to data, remember to check the exact meaning of the data that you are using. It is easy to forget to do this.

PRACTICE QUESTIONS

Data response question

1   a   Using the data in Figure 40.1, compare Malaysia's productivity positions with those of South Korea and Japan.
    b   Explain **two** possible reasons for the differences you have observed.

WORKED EXAMPLE FOR Q1

a   Malaysia's productivity per employee in 2018 is slightly below the levels of Korea and Japan. Malaysia's average productivity growth from 2001–2018 is much higher than productivity growth in Korea and Japan **[A]**.

b   Malaysia's productivity growth has come about due to the accumulation of capital resources and the discovery and exploitation of oil and gas. More of South Korea's and Japan's productivity growth could have come from a better-quality labour resource **[A]**.

Essay questions

1   Evaluate the extent to which transfer earnings and economic rent can be used to explain the difference in earnings between the chief executive of a multinational company and one of its local managers.
2   Assess the view that imperfect labour markets never benefit the employment of workers, but only benefit those who employ them.

Improve this answer

This is a sample answer to essay Q1.

> Transfer earnings and economic rent are concepts that can be used to explain why some people are paid more than others. If you take the case of a firm, it is obvious that the head of a huge company is going to get paid more than someone who is just managing a small part of the company.
>
> Economic rent is the term that is used for the payment that is made to someone as a basic payment for them to remain in an occupation. It is the amount that keeps a person happy to continue in work with that firm or organisation. If they are not paid this minimum amount, they will look for work elsewhere. Transfer earnings are what they receive in the form of additional wages when they get promoted to a better job.
>
> The head of the company is paid well because it is likely that this person will have been well educated and will need to work long hours. As head of an organisation, high pay compensates for risks that have to be taken. Star soccer players like Lionel Messi are incredibly well paid for their unique talent. Their labour supply curve is a vertical line **[K]**.

CONTINUED

Your challenge

See whether you can improve this answer. This answer is poor. The first and final paragraphs contain some basic description. The second paragraph includes material that is wrong. There is total confusion over the difference between transfer earnings and economic rent, the fundamental point of the question. An assessment like this needs a diagram that is then analysed. There is no evaluation. A better answer is given in the workbook answers – but write yours out first.

Unit 9
The macroeconomy (A Level)

Chapter 41
The circular flow of income

LEARNING INTENTIONS

In this chapter you will:

- explain the meaning of the multiplier
- calculate the multiplier using formulae in a closed economy without a government sector, a closed economy with a government sector and an open economy with a government sector
- calculate the average and marginal propensities to save, consume and import
- calculate the average and marginal rates of tax
- analyse how national income is determined, using aggregate demand and income approach
- calculate the effect of changing aggregate demand on national income using the multiplier
- describe the determinants of aggregate demand
- explain the consumption function: autonomous and induced consumer expenditure
- explain the savings function: autonomous and induced savings
- explain the determinants of investment
- explain the difference between autonomous and induced investment
- explain the meaning of the accelerator
- analyse the determinants of government spending
- describe the determinants of net exports
- explain the relationship between the full employment level of national income and the equilibrium level of national income
- analyse inflationary and deflationary gaps.

KEY TERMS

Accelerator theory   Aggregate expenditure   Autonomous investment   Average propensity to consume (apc)
Average propensity to import (apm)   Average propensity to save (aps)   Average rate of tax (art)   Capital–output ratio
Closed economy   Consumption   Consumption function   Deflationary gap   Disposable income   Dissaving
Government spending   Induced investment   Inflationary gap   Investment   Marginal propensity to consume (mpc)
Marginal propensity to import (mpm)   Marginal propensity to save (mps)   Marginal rate of tax (mrt)   Multiplier
Net exports   Open economy   Saving   Savings function

Key skills exercises

Knowledge and understanding

To answer the questions in this chapter, you need to know and understand:

- the meaning of the multiplier and how it is calculated
- how national income is determined, using the aggregate demand and income approach with the multiplier process
- the effect of changing aggregate demand on national income using the multiplier
- the consumption function: autonomous and induced consumer expenditure

- the savings function: autonomous and induced savings
- what determines investment
- the difference between autonomous and induced investment
- the accelerator theory
- the determinants of net exports
- the difference between inflationary and deflationary gaps.

1 Explain the multiplier process.
2 How is the multiplier calculated?
3 Differentiate between a closed economy and an open economy.
4 What is meant by aggregate expenditure?
5 Explain what determines consumption.
6 Explain the difference between autonomous and induced consumer expenditure.
7 Explain what determines investment.
8 Explain the difference between autonomous and induced investment.
9 Explain the accelerator process.
10 What are the determinants of net exports?
11 Explain the difference between an inflationary gap and a deflationary gap.

Analysis

Tourism multipliers: measuring the economic impact of tourism

Tourism is an important source of income and employment in many countries. Tourism's economic impact can be measured through the multiplier. Figure 41.1 shows the impact of UK tourist spending in euros (€) across the European Union (EU).

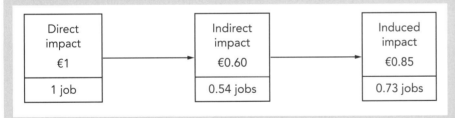

Figure 41.1: The impact of a UK tourist spending in the EU

Across the EU, the tourist income multiplier was estimated to be 2.46. The employment multiplier was 2.27.

The size of both multipliers varied across the EU's member states. For example, in Spain, the tourist income multiplier was 2.98, yet in Luxembourg it was 1.67. The employment multipliers were 3.65 for Spain and 1.87 for Luxembourg.

Tourism's economic impact is usually even greater in low-income countries. In South Africa, for example, it has been estimated that for every night a tourist stays in a 'high-end game lodge', 14 people in the surrounding area benefit.

12 In an open economy, mps is 0.1, the mrt is 0.15 and the mpm is 0.15:
   a Calculate the value of the multiplier.
   b Calculate the final change in income when there is an increase of $100m in private sector investment.
13 Using the data in Figure 41.1, analyse the ways in which UK tourist spending impacts on the economies of EU member states.
14 Explain the likely reasons for the difference in the tourism income multipliers for Spain and for Luxembourg.

WORKED EXAMPLE FOR Q14

The best way to answer this question is to use the multiplier formula:

$$K = \frac{1}{mps + mrt + mpm}$$

The higher value for Spain is due to there being less leakages from the circular flow of income. For Luxembourg, leakages will be a greater proportion of income. Due to Luxembourg being a small country, the leakages from imports are likely to mean that the mpm is high [A].

TIP

Most learners do not appreciate that very few real-world studies have been made to calculate the value of the multiplier. A general conclusion is that for most economies, the multiplier is low, typically around 1.3. In a very open economy the multiplier could even be below 1.

15 Explain the likely reason for the employment multiplier in Spain to be bigger than the income multiplier.
16 Assuming a multiplier of 2, analyse the impact of a cut in government spending on national income.

Evaluation

17 Comment on the benefits and costs of 'high-end game lodge' tourism for South Africa's economy.

41 The circular flow of income

PRACTICE QUESTIONS

Multiple-choice question

1 The multiplier in an economy is 4. The mps is 0.1 and the mrt is 0.05. The value of mpm is:

A 0.05

B 0.1

C 0.15

D 0.25

Essay questions

1 An economy experiences a rise in consumer spending.

Evaluate the extent to which the final impact on national income depends upon the size of the multiplier.

2 Assess the factors that affect a change in net exports and how this impacts on the circular flow of income in an economy.

Improve this answer

This is a sample answer to essay Q2.

> Exports are goods and services that are sold by one country to another country. Imports are the goods and services that are purchased from all other countries. The term 'net exports' is the difference between exports and imports. Within the circular flow of income, exports are an injection while imports are a withdrawal. So, if net exports increase, this represents an increase in the circular flow of income, a decrease in net exports is a decrease in the circular flow of income [K].
>
> It will be useful to explain what determines net exports. Much depends on price, especially the competitiveness of one country's prices compared to its main trading competitors. If an exporting country is experiencing high inflation, there is a danger that its exports will reduce in competitiveness compared to rival producers. Much will depend on the price elasticity of demand for exports [A]. The likelihood, though, is that the value of exports may fall.
>
> Other factors need to be considered. The quality of exports is important when trading agricultural products and some types of manufactured goods. Another factor which can be crucial is the foreign exchange rate of the exporter and the country that is purchasing exports. A depreciating exchange rate for the exporting country relative to the importer's exchange rate should produce a positive outcome for export sales. The negative side to this is that a depreciating exchange rate could increase domestic inflation which in turn could have a detrimental effect on the price competitiveness of exports [A]. This is particularly relevant where the manufactured exports of a country are dependent on imported supplies.
>
> As shown above, there are various factors that affect a change in net exports. Price is arguably the most important. An increase in net exports increases the circular flow of income, a decrease in net exports reduces the circular flow of income [E]

Your challenge

See whether you can improve this answer. The answer has the foundation to become a better answer. The first paragraph is descriptive and could be shortened. This will allow more time to analyse the significance of GDP and barriers to trade in those countries that are an economy's trading partners. The current final paragraph could be rewritten to include more evaluation and a new final paragraph added. Your challenge is to write a new first paragraph and two concluding paragraphs. A better answer is given in the workbook answers – but write yours out first.

Chapter 42
Economic growth and sustainability

LEARNING INTENTIONS

In this chapter you will:
- explain the difference between actual growth and potential growth in national output
- explain the causes and consequences of positive and negative output gaps
- describe the phases of the business (trade) cycle
- analyse the causes of the business cycle
- explain the role of automatic stabilisers
- evaluate the effectiveness of policies to promote economic growth
- explain the meaning of inclusive economic growth
- analyse the impact of economic growth on equity and equality
- analyse policies to promote inclusive economic growth
- explain the meaning of sustainable economic growth
- explain the difference between using and conserving resources
- analyse the impact of economic growth on the environment and climate change
- evaluate the policies to mitigate the impact of economic growth on the environment and climate change.

KEY TERMS

Actual economic growth   Automatic stabilisers   Business cycle   Climate change   Depression
Gig economy   Global warming   Greenhouse gases   Negative output gap   Output gap   Polluter pays principle
Positive output gap   Potential economic growth   Supply-side shocks   Sustainable economic growth

Key skills exercises

Knowledge and understanding

To answer the questions in this chapter, you need to know and understand:
- the difference between actual growth and potential growth
- the causes and consequences of output gaps
- the phases and causes of the business cycle
- the role of automatic stabilisers
- policies to promote economic growth
- the meaning of inclusive economic growth
- the impact of economic growth on equity and equality
- the policies to promote inclusive economic growth

42 Economic growth and sustainability

- the meaning of sustainable economic growth
- using and conserving resources
- the impact of economic growth on the environment and climate change
- policies to mitigate the impact of economic growth on the environment and climate change.

1. Describe the difference between actual growth and potential growth.
2. Describe what is meant by an output gap.
3. Describe the phases and causes of the business cycle.
4. Explain the meaning of inclusive economic growth.
5. Explain the meaning of sustainable economic growth.
6. Explain the difference between using and conserving resources.

> **TIP**
>
> When writing about the downturn in the business cycle caused by the COVID-19 pandemic, consider whether the change in real GDP has followed an L, U, V or W shaped recovery over time.

Analysis

> **Inclusive and sustainable economic growth in Azerbaijan**
>
> Azerbaijan, the former Soviet republic, has consistently recorded the highest rate of economic growth of any country this century. From 2004 to 2015, Azerbaijan's annual growth rate averaged 10.6%. Since then, GDP per head has been stable. Azerbaijan is now classified as an upper middle-income country.
>
> Azerbaijan's spectacular growth can be summed up in one world – oil. Its economy received a boost with the opening of the Baku–Tbilisi–Ceyhan pipeline in 2005. The fall in the global price of oil and the need to reduce dependence on oil have prompted Azerbaijan's government to diversify the economy. This has involved developing the non-oil sector, especially agriculture, and promoting a competitive market where small and medium enterprises (SMEs) can flourish. The strategy for agriculture has been to export high-value products such as pomegranates and hazelnuts, for which Azerbaijan has a comparative advantage.
>
> The most noteworthy point about Azerbaijan's development plans has been the government's long-term commitment to inclusive and sustainable growth. The government is determined to develop its future workforce through improved education, work experience and training. It is also keen to promote women's entrepreneurship. Azerbaijan's government works with commercial banks to provide assistance, advice and loans for SMEs. The aim is to allow entrepreneurs to expand their businesses to generate sustainable economic growth for Azerbaijan.

7. Analyse how automatic stabilisers can reduce fluctuations in GDP.
8. Explain how Azerbaijan has sought to promote inclusive economic growth.
9. Explain how Azerbaijan has sought to promote sustainable economic growth.
10. Analyse the likely impact of the business cycle on Azerbaijan's economic growth rate.

WORKED EXAMPLE FOR Q10

Although there is only limited information on Azerbaijan's annual growth rates, it is most likely that the opening of the Baku–Tbilisi–Ceyhan pipeline in 2005 led to an upturn in the economy's business cycle. A peak was likely to have been reached in 2008 to be followed by a downturn due to the global financial crisis. This crisis would put the business cycle in the trough phase [A].

The business cycle is likely to have continued until the downturn in the global economy in 2012. More recently, the business cycle appears to be less obvious than in the early part of the century. Automatic stabilisers are likely to have been in evidence [A].

Evaluation

11 Comment on the extent to which Azerbaijan's development policy mitigates the impact on the environment and climate change.

PRACTICE QUESTIONS

Multiple-choice question

1 Which of these ways of producing more electricity is likely to be most sustainable?

    A a new wind farm

    B a new gas-fired power station

    C a new coal-fired power station

    D a new nuclear reactor

Essay questions

1 Assess the extent to which it is realistic for middle-income countries to promote inclusive and sustainable economic growth at the same time.

2 Evaluate the view that it is not possible for economic growth to take place without a net increase in resources.

Improve this answer

This is a sample answer to essay Q2.

> Economic growth occurs when there is an increase in the real GDP in an economy. This is usually indicated by an annual increase in output. It is represented by a shift outwards of an economy's PPC, indicating that more of both goods can now be produced. For an economy's people to benefit from this growth, the rate of population growth must be less than the increase in real output. Economic growth is an objective of virtually all economies, although there are growing concerns that growth should be more sustainable in terms of the resources being used **[K]**.
>
> Economic growth can occur through an increase in either the quantity or quality of resources available. For example, in terms of quantity, an economy may benefit from an increase in population or an increase in the number of people willing to take risks as entrepreneurs. For some economies, such as some Middle Eastern ones, migrant labour has led to an increase in growth. An improvement in the quality of resources is also important for growth to be achieved **[K]**.
>
> Those countries, such as China, India, South Korea and Vietnam, that have achieved high rates of growth have done so through deliberately increasing investment and promoting export-led growth. Both policies have required an increase in resources to be devoted to growth. One of the costs of this approach is that there is a danger that current consumption is being held back since resources are being put into new public and private sector investment **[A]**. On a more positive note, in China especially, there is a long tradition of a high savings rate. This has helped to promote investment.
>
> Investment requires resources to be put into building new roads, factories, power supplies and into making agriculture more productive to meet the needs of an expanding population. It is really very difficult to see how this can come about when there is no net increase in resources **[A]**.

Your challenge

See whether you can improve this answer. The answer is superficial and lacks depth of analysis. The issue of quality of resources, for example, is not developed. The final paragraph only touches on the point of the question. This paragraph should refer back to the point of the question, namely to evaluate whether it is possible for economic growth to occur without a net use of resources. A better answer is given in the workbook answers – but write yours out first.

Chapter 43
Employment and unemployment

LEARNING INTENTIONS

In this chapter you will:
- define the meaning of full employment
- explain the difference between equilibrium and disequilibrium unemployment
- explain the difference between voluntary and involuntary unemployment
- define the meaning of the natural rate of unemployment
- explain the determinants of the natural rate of unemployment
- analyse the policy implications of the natural rate of unemployment
- describe patterns and trends in (un)employment
- explain the forms of labour mobility: geographical and occupational
- analyse the factors affecting labour mobility
- evaluate the effectiveness of policies to reduce unemployment.

KEY TERMS

Disequilibrium unemployment   Equilibrium unemployment   Full employment   Geographical mobility of labour   Hysteresis   Informal economy   Long-term unemployment   Natural rate of unemployment   Occupational mobility of labour   Self-employed   Voluntary unemployment

Key skills exercises

To answer the questions in this chapter, you need to know and understand:
- what is meant by full employment
- the difference between equilibrium and disequilibrium unemployment
- the difference between voluntary and involuntary unemployment
- the meaning of the natural rate of unemployment
- the policy implications of the natural rate of unemployment (including hysteresis)
- how to describe patterns and trends in unemployment and employment
- the forms of labour mobility
- the factors affecting labour mobility
- the policies that can be applied to reduce unemployment.

1   Define full employment.
2   Explain the difference between equilibrium and disequilibrium unemployment.

3   Define the natural rate of unemployment.

4   Explain what determines the natural rate of unemployment.

5   Explain the difference between voluntary and involuntary unemployment.

6   Explain the types of labour mobility.

Analysis

Youth unemployment in Brunei

Unemployment rates in ASEAN member states were at an all-time low in 2018. The exception was Brunei, where its rate of unemployment was almost double that of any other member state (see Figure 43.1).

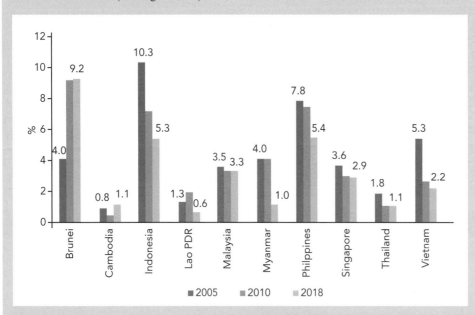

Figure 43.1: Unemployment rates (%) by ASEAN Member States, 2005–2018

Source: ASEANstats database

Brunei's high rate of unemployment was due to the youth unemployment rate, which in 2017 was 28.9%, and highlighted in a report by the International Monetary Fund (IMF). The report identified the need to reduce youth unemployment. The IMF believed that strong economic growth and structural reform of the labour market were necessary for the youth unemployment rate to be reduced. A failure to tackle this problem would lead to the outward migration of skilled labour.

The IMF report was critical of the vocational training provided in Brunei. It noted that the highest levels of youth unemployment were among those who had a vocational background. The IMF stressed that the quality of vocational training needed to change to reduce current skill mismatches.

The IMF also recognised that youth unemployment was more sensitive to economic growth than adult unemployment due to the concentration of jobs in those parts of the economy most likely to be affected by the business cycle.

> **TIP**
>
> International comparisons of unemployment rates should be handled with care. This is due to variations in the methods of collection and interpretation of the definition of when someone is unemployed.

43 Employment and unemployment

7 Compare the unemployment rates of Malaysia and Vietnam from 2005 to 2018.

8 Analyse how youth unemployment is affected by economic growth in Brunei.

9 Analyse how structural reform of the labour market might reduce youth unemployment in Brunei.

10 Analyse the costs of youth emigration from Brunei to other ASEAN member states.

Evaluation

11 Comment upon the factors that might have been responsible for fluctuations in the unemployment rates of ASEAN member states from 2005 to 2018.

PRACTICE QUESTIONS

Data response question

1 Using the data in Figure 43.1, explain **two** reasons why the accuracy of the statistics is likely to be variable.

WORKED EXAMPLE FOR Q1

It is highly likely that the unemployment rate data is variable in its accuracy. The size of the labour market in Indonesia is huge compared to Singapore, and there is likely to be a bigger informal economy where people work on an irregular basis and may not have a registered job [A]. There are also variations in the proportion of women in the labour force, due to differing attitudes towards women's role in society and the economy [A].

Essay questions

1 Assess whether demand-side or supply-side policies are likely to be best for reducing unemployment in middle-income countries.

2 Evaluate the policies that a government might use to reduce the natural rate of unemployment.

Improve this answer

This is a sample answer to essay Q1.

> Unemployment is a situation where someone who is willing and able to work is without a job. Unemployment is found in all types of economy, low-, middle- and high-income countries. Particularly in low- and middle-income economies, the official figures for those people out of work could be misleading. Especially in low-income and lower middle-income countries, underemployment is common. Other workers may not be classed as unemployed if they are part of the informal economy [K].
>
> The policies for reducing unemployment depend to a large extent on the reason or reasons why someone is unemployed. Taking the case of cyclical unemployment, since this is due to a lack of aggregate demand, it is appropriate for a government to use policies to increase aggregate demand. Expansionary fiscal and monetary policies are appropriate. An increase in government spending on new roads, water supplies and electricity is a positive way of increasing employment. Government spending like this will have a ripple or multiplier impact throughout the economy, leading to further job creation [A].

CONTINUED

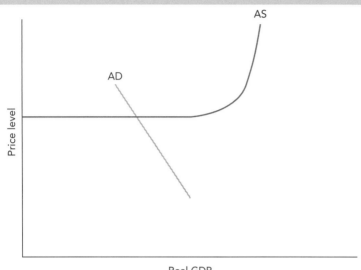

If unemployment is caused through the changing structure of an economy, then supply-side policies are more appropriate in reducing unemployment. If someone who has worked in the coal industry, steel industry and agriculture is unemployed, it is unlikely that they will have the skills needed to get another job in one of the emerging sectors of the economy, like electronics and computer engineering. Supply-side policies can provide training in the skills required for employment in a more modern economy **[A]**.

It is much easier to reduce unemployment where this is caused by frictional factors. A government can make sure that more job information is available. It is also a good idea for the government to take a critical look at unemployment and other benefits as they may sometimes, if high, do little to tempt an unemployed worker to return to employment **[A]**.

Your challenge

See whether you can improve this answer. The answer contains some relevant information but, overall, it is superficial and lacks a conclusion. Two other areas for improvement are that monetary policies are not explained. The diagram serves little or no purpose. There also needs to be more focus on middle-income countries. A better answer is given in the workbook answers – but write yours out first.

Chapter 44
Money and banking

LEARNING INTENTIONS

In this chapter you will:
- define the meaning of money
- explain the functions and characteristics of money
- define the meaning of money supply
- analyse the quantity theory of money
- explain the functions of commercial banks, including providing deposit accounts; lending money; holding or providing cash, securities, loans, deposits, equity; reserve ratio and capital ratio; the objectives of commercial banks
- analyse the causes of changes in the money supply in an open economy, including credit creation, government deficit financing, quantitative easing, change in the balance of payments
- explain the role of the bank credit multiplier
- explain the role of the central bank
- evaluate the effectiveness of policies to reduce inflation
- explain demand for money (liquidity preference theory)
- evaluate interest rate determination according to both the loanable funds theory and the Keynesian theory.

KEY TERMS

Active balances   Bank credit multiplier   Broad money   Capital ratio   Commercial banks
Demand deposit account   Double coincidence of wants   Economic and monetary union   Equities   Fisher equation
Government securities   Idle balances   Liquidity   Liquidity preference   Liquidity trap   Loan   Money
Money supply   Narrow money   Overdraft   Precautionary motive   Quantitative easing   Quantity theory of money
Reserve ratio   Savings deposit account   Speculative motive   Total currency flow   Transactions motive

Key skills exercises

Knowledge and understanding

To answer the questions in this chapter, you need to know and understand:
- the functions and characteristics of money
- the money supply
- the quantity theory of money
- Keynesian and monetarist theoretical approaches
- the functions and objectives of commercial banks
- the causes of changes in the money supply, including the bank credit multiplier
- the role of a central bank
- the effectiveness of policies to reduce inflation
- the liquidity preference theory
- interest rate determination, including loanable funds theory.

1. Describe the functions and characteristics of money.
2. Explain the difference between narrow money and broad money.
3. Explain the quantity theory of money.
4. Explain the bank credit multiplier process.
5. Explain how quantitative easing works.
6. Explain liquidity preference theory.
7. Explain what is meant by 'helicopter money'.

Analysis

> **'Helicopter money' to the rescue?**
>
> In response to the COVID-19 pandemic, the US administration responded with a $2 trillion rescue deal. This included loans, aid to small businesses and healthcare providers and, significantly, direct payments to individuals.
>
> For those earning less than $99 000 a year (double for couples), the package provided a direct payment by bank cheque for $1200 plus $500 for each child. In addition, unemployment benefit was boosted by $600 per week and eligibility extended to cover more workers.
>
> The direct payments to individual Americans are an example of 'helicopter money', a term coined by the monetary economist Milton Friedman. Its purpose is to produce a one-off universal cash injection to stimulate consumer spending in order to get an economy out of deep recession.
>
> Unlike fiscal and monetary policies, direct payments are designed to produce a quick impact. Families affected by unemployment can use the helicopter money to pay mortgages and buy groceries. This is fine in principle. The principle comes unstuck when individuals save the helicopter money rather than spend it. This reduces the impact on aggregate demand and reduces output to what it would otherwise have been, reducing employment.

8. Analyse how the payment of helicopter money in the USA affected the supply of money.

WORKED EXAMPLE FOR Q8

The aim of helicopter money is to provide an immediate increase in the money supply to prompt those receiving it to go out and spend it and allow the economy to move out of recession [A].

9. Analyse reasons for a change in the money supply.

Evaluation

10. Discuss the extent to which helicopter money alone might be able to move the US economy out of deep recession.

PRACTICE QUESTIONS

Multiple-choice question

1. The rate of interest in some countries has been negative. Which of these is true?
   - **A** The rate of inflation is negative.
   - **B** The real value of savers' deposits is falling.
   - **C** The cost of borrowing from banks is negative.
   - **D** There is an urgent need to reduce aggregate demand.

Essay questions

1. Evaluate interest rate determination according to the loanable funds and Keynesian theories.
2. Assess the effectiveness of the ways in which government and central bank policies are able to reduce inflation in an economy.

Improve this answer

This is a sample answer to essay Q2.

> Inflation is a situation where there is a sustained increase in the price level in an economy. The level of inflation varies between economies, and for this reason a policy that might be applied in one economy may not be entirely appropriate for combating inflation in another economy.
>
> There are two main groups of policy used to reduce inflation. They are contractionary monetary policy and deflationary fiscal policy. Both are likely to be used at the same time. These policies involve reducing the money supply and in the case of fiscal policy, cutting back on government spending or increasing taxation or a mixture of both. Supply-side policies could be used to control cost-push inflation although these policies will take time to have an effect **[K]**.
>
> Getting the best policy is potentially difficult. It will also depend on the relationship between a government and its central bank, especially if the bank has a particular degree of independence. The nature of inflation in an economy is that inflation is usually caused by more than one factor. So, demand-pull and cost-push causes combine to increase in price level. A further complication is where a depreciation in the exchange rate causes inflation – this type of cost-push inflation cannot always be corrected by domestic policies.
>
> Suppose inflation is primarily caused by an increase in the money supply. A reason for this could be due to quantitative easing when interest rates are low. The intention behind quantitative easing is to encourage the commercial banks to lend more money to businesses. If too much lending is agreed by commercial banks, the danger is that the rate of inflation is likely to accelerate, so off-setting the purpose of quantitative easing. **[A]**
>
> One of the big unknowns in economic policy is how firms and households will respond to policies to reduce inflation. Suppose there is a rise in the rate of interest. Consumers could respond by not reducing their consumption as they fear that further price increases could follow. Another example could be in the case of an increase in income tax. Consumers could work longer hours to maintain living standards or they could draw upon savings, both of which will increase aggregate demand at a time when the most appropriate policy is to reduce aggregate demand. **[A]**

Your challenge

See whether you can improve this answer. The answer shows an understanding of the point of the question. However, less focus could have been spent on the first two paragraphs, which are contextual and could be shortened. Your challenge is to produce a brief opening paragraph, a paragraph with more examples and a concluding paragraph. A better answer is given in the workbook answers – but write yours out first.

> Unit 10

Government macroeconomic intervention (A Level)

> Chapter 45

Government macroeconomic policy objectives

LEARNING INTENTIONS

In this chapter you will:

- analyse macroeconomic policy objectives in terms of inflation, balance of payments, unemployment, growth, development, sustainability and redistribution of income and wealth.

KEY TERMS

Labour force participation rate   Sustainable development

Key skills exercises

Knowledge and understanding

To answer the questions in this chapter, you need to know and understand:

- the meaning of low and stable inflation
- balance of payments stability
- low unemployment
- sustained economic growth
- economic development
- the meaning of sustainable development
- how to redistribute income and wealth.

1. Explain what is meant by low and stable inflation.
2. Explain what is meant by balance of payments stability.
3. Explain the meaning of low unemployment.
4. Explain the meaning of sustained economic growth.
5. Explain what is meant by sustainable development
6. Explain what is meant by the redistribution of income and wealth.

WORKED EXAMPLE FOR Q6

The redistribution of income and wealth occurs when, as a consequence of government policies, there is a more equitable distribution amongst the population. **[K]**

Analysis

South Korea: Asia's powerhouse

South Korea is now a high-income country with a GDP per head of around $26 000 in 2019. The economy has been transformed through sustained economic growth. Successive governments have supported domestic industries. The privatisation of former state-owned industries was designed to protect family-owned businesses from outside competition, a policy known as *chaebol*. Unlike other Asian countries, multinational companies (MNCs) were not allowed to bid for the nationalised industries.

Figure 45.1 shows an assessment made in 2019 of South Korea's economic policies.

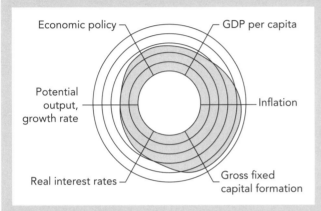

Figure 45.1: Spider chart showing the success of South Korea's economic policies

Source: Bertelsmann Stiftung

South Korea's macroeconomic policy objectives are:
- moderate, stable economic growth
- maintaining a current account surplus on the balance of payments
- a healthy rate of inflation
- low interest rates
- low tax rates
- low, stable unemployment.

South Korea does have policy challenges. Some are:
- to reduce youth unemployment
- to reform the labour market by making more jobs permanent
- to reduce consumer debt.

7 Analyse how low interest rates in South Korea may lead to increased economic growth.

8 Analyse how low interest rates in South Korea might affect other macroeconomic policy objectives.

9 Analyse how supply-side policies might be used to combat South Korea's labour market challenges.

Evaluation

10 Using the information in Figure 45.1, discuss South Korea's recent economic performance.

PRACTICE QUESTIONS

Multiple-choice question

1. The annual rate of inflation in an economy is stable at 5% over a two-year period.

    Which of these is true?

    A   There is no change in the price level over the two-year period.

    B   The rate of inflation is low in each of the two years.

    C   The price level is higher at the end of the two-year period.

    D   The prices that increased in the first year also increased by the same amount in the second year.

Essay questions

1. 'Economic growth is a primary objective of many governments but it cannot guarantee a rising level of economic development.'

    Evaluate this statement.

2. Assess whether maintaining a low rate of unemployment should always be the number one objective of macroeconomic policy.

Improve this answer

This is a sample answer to essay Q2.

> Unemployment is a situation where there are people who are willing and able to work but who do not have a job. Unemployment is an issue in all economies. It is one of a series of macroeconomic objectives that governments have **[K]**.
>
> Unemployment is not good for the economy or for those who do not have a job. For the economy, it means that there is spare capacity – unemployed workers could in principle be contributing more output. For an individual who is unemployed, there are financial and personal implications. Government benefits are not a substitute for a fair rate of pay from a job.
>
> Another objective of the government is to control inflation. This is also important since high inflation can make domestic exports uncompetitive. A high rate of inflation also undermines household income, meaning that less can be bought with a fixed level of income. The problem with inflation is that it can destroy confidence and lead to other problems.
>
> A third objective of economies is that of economic growth. This is the ultimate objective in some respects since growth provides for an increase in living standards. All economies are striving to provide this for their respective populations.
>
> A final objective is to keep a balance in the balance of payments. This is often difficult, especially for developing economies which rely on imports, but often have unstable export revenue. A run of deficits in the balance of trade has eventually to be paid for. It often means that a country is forced to borrow money to pay off the debts from imports. **[K]**

Your challenge

See whether you can improve this answer. This is a weak answer, although it considers four areas of macroeconomic policy. The content is general and fails to recognise that in terms of objectives there needs to be a more precise explanation. The explanation should be analytical. A conclusion is required to provide an assessment of the extent to which a low rate of unemployment should be the number one objective of macroeconomic policy. A better answer is given in the workbook answers – but write yours out first.

> Chapter 46
Links between macroeconomic problems and their interrelatedness

LEARNING INTENTIONS

In this chapter you will:

- describe the relationship between the internal value of money and the external value of money
- explain the relationship between the balance of payments and inflation
- explain the relationship between growth and inflation
- explain the relationship between growth and the balance of payments
- explain the relationship between inflation and unemployment
- analyse the traditional Phillips cure
- explain the expectations-augmented Phillips curve (short-and long-run Phillips curve).

KEY TERMS

Expectations-augmented Phillips curve   Phillips curve

Key skills exercises

Knowledge and understanding

To answer the questions in this chapter, you need to know and understand:

- the relationship between the internal value of money and the external value of money
- the relationship between the balance of payments and inflation
- the relationship between growth and inflation
- the relationship between growth and the balance of payments
- the relationship between inflation and unemployment
- what is shown by the traditional Phillips curve
- what is shown by the expectations-augmented Phillips curve.

TIP

The relationships identified in this chapter are relevant for an assessment of the effectiveness of the extent to which a government is meeting its macroeconomic objectives.

1 Describe the relationship between the internal value of money and the external value of money (currency).

> ## WORKED EXAMPLE FOR Q1
>
> The internal value of money refers to the goods and services that can be bought by a unit of currency at any one time. Inflation will reduce the value of money since less can be bought with each dollar/rupee or other unit of currency. The external value of money is the international exchange rate of a currency **[K]**.
>
> The internal and external values of money are closely related. For example, if a country is experiencing a high rate of inflation, its exports may become less price competitive. The demand for its currency will fall, causing its exchange rate to depreciate. The knock-on effect of this is that the price of imports will increase, leading to a fall in the value of the domestic currency. So, a fall in the internal value of money leads to a fall in the external value of money. Likewise an increase in the value of money will lead to an increase in the currency's foreign exchange rate **[K]**.

2 Explain the relationship between the balance of payments and inflation.

3 Explain the relationship between growth and inflation.

4 Explain the relationship between growth and the balance of payments.

5 Explain the relationship between inflation and unemployment.

6 Explain what is shown by the traditional Phillips curve.

7 Explain what is shown by the expectations-augmented Phillips curve.

Analysis

> **What has happened to the Phillips curve?**
>
> The relationship between inflation and unemployment is one that has long fascinated economists. This relationship was first modelled by the economist A.W. Phillips over 50 years ago. The Phillips curve in its basic form shows that if the labour market is tight, with low unemployment, wages will increase at a faster rate than when there is a high level of unemployment.
>
> Figure 46.1 shows the results of an empirical study of the US economy from 1998 to the end of 2017. Average wage growth has been unusually slow since 2010 in the USA.
>
> There is little doubt that the relationship between unemployment and earnings has changed. Monetary economists believe that there is no long-term relationship – the relationship is now just short-term. New Keynesian economists disagree. They are standing by the relationship, but are now saying that the relationship is between the volatility of prices and deviations of unemployment from the natural rate of unemployment.
>
> A casualty of this academic debate is government macroeconomic policy. The Phillips curve was used to establish a trade-off between unemployment and the level of inflation, especially where a government had set targets for each. This would no longer appear feasible.

46 Links between macroeconomic problems and their interrelatedness

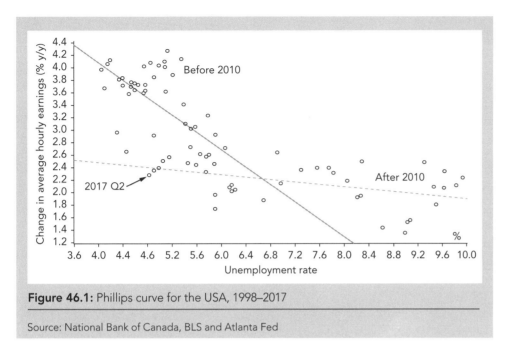

Figure 46.1: Phillips curve for the USA, 1998–2017

Source: National Bank of Canada, BLS and Atlanta Fed

8 Using the data in Figure 46.1, outline the relationships between the unemployment rate and average hourly earnings growth in the USA before 2010.

9 Explain how this relationship changed after 2010.

Evaluation

10 Comment on the value of the information in Figure 46.1 to macroeconomic policymakers in the USA.

PRACTICE QUESTIONS

Multiple-choice question

1 The table below gives an economy's unemployment rate and inflation rate for a five-year period.

Year	Unemployment rate %	Inflation rate %
2016	8.2	3.1
2017	6.9	2.8
2018	6.3	3.0
2019	6.6	3.2
2020	6.2	3.2

Which change between consecutive years is consistent with the underlying principle of the Phillips curve?

A 2016–2017

B 2017–2018

C 2018–2019

D 2019–2020

CONTINUED

Essay questions

1 Assess whether a government might be able to sustain a macroeconomic policy that at the same time promotes low unemployment and low inflation.
2 Evaluate whether an increase in the rate of inflation in an economy is likely to cause more harm to the balance of payments than to economic growth.

Improve this answer

This is a sample answer to essay Q2.

> An increase in the rate of inflation affects the balance of payments in various ways. When the prices of domestic-produced goods, including exports, increase due to rising costs, there is likely to be an effect on international competitiveness. An increase in the price of a country's exports could mean that they become less competitive compared to the same or similar products from other countries. The extent of the change in the demand will depend on the price elasticity of demand for these exports. In turn, this will affect the balance of trade of a country.
>
> The balance of trade can also be affected by an increase in imports of goods and services which are now relatively cheaper due to an increase in the rate of inflation. Again, the impact will depend on the price elasticity of demand for imports. Any rise in import spending will result in the current account balance deteriorating **[A]**.
>
> Another link between the rate of inflation and the balance of payments is if net exports of a country increase. This will boost aggregate demand and may increase or lead to a surplus in the balance of trade and current account of the balance of payments. If the surplus in the current account is prolonged, the exchange rate will increase. Exports will become less competitive and imports more competitive. The final effect is likely to be a reduction in the current account balance **[A]**.
>
> The link between the rate of inflation and economic growth is not as obvious. As noted earlier, an increase in the rate of inflation is likely to see a fall in a country's net exports. This will therefore reduce aggregate demand and output. This in turn will reduce the rate of growth if the reduction in output is sustained. So, export-led growth is likely to be affected by an increase in the rate of inflation **[E]**.

Your challenge

See whether you can improve this answer. The answer is unbalanced. More needs to be written on the relationship between inflation and economic growth. Also, the question has barely been addressed in terms of a judgement on whether an increase in the rate of inflation causes more harm to the balance of payments or to economic growth. Your challenge is to add two final paragraphs. A better answer is given in the workbook answers – but write yours out first.

> Chapter 47
Effectiveness of policy options to meet all macroeconomic objectives

LEARNING INTENTIONS

In this chapter you will:

- evaluate the effectiveness of fiscal policy including Laffer curve analysis in relation to different macroeconomic objectives
- evaluate the effectiveness of monetary policy in relation to different macroeconomic objectives
- evaluate the effectiveness of supply-side policy in relation to different macroeconomic objectives
- evaluate the effectiveness of exchange rate policy in relation to different macroeconomic objectives
- evaluate the effectiveness of international trade policy in relation to different macroeconomic objectives
- analyse problems and conflicts arising from the outcome of the different policies
- explain the existence of government failure in macroeconomic policies.

KEY TERMS

Counter-cyclically   Crowding in   Crowding out   Government macroeconomic failure   Laffer curve

Key skills exercises

Knowledge and understanding

To answer the questions in this chapter, you need to know and understand:

- how fiscal policy relates to different macroeconomic policy objectives
- the features of a Laffer curve
- how monetary policy relates to different macroeconomic policy objectives
- how supply-side policies relate to different macroeconomic policy objectives
- how exchange rate policy relates to different macroeconomic policy objectives
- how international trade policy relates to different macroeconomic policy objectives
- the problems and conflicts that arise from the outcome of different policy objectives
- government failure in macroeconomic policies.

1   Explain what is shown by a Laffer curve.
2   Explain how fiscal policy relates to different macroeconomic objectives.

WORKED EXAMPLE FOR Q2

An expansionary fiscal policy involves an increase in government spending, a reduction in taxation or a combination of both. The purpose of the policy is to boost aggregate demand and so reduce the level of unemployment. An increase in economic growth may also occur. However, there is a danger that the increase in aggregate demand could lead to demand-pull inflation and a reduction in net exports [A].

3   Explain how monetary policy relates to different macroeconomic policy objectives.
4   Explain how supply-side policies relate to different macroeconomic policy objectives.
5   Explain how exchange rate policy relates to different macroeconomic policy objectives.
6   Explain how international trade policy relates to different macroeconomic policy objectives.

Analysis

Pakistan's economy is on the right track

In April 2020, a report from the Asian Development Bank (ADB) provided some good news on Pakistan's economy. The report recognised that stabilisation policies were providing a positive contribution to the domestic economy and to reducing the deficit on the current account of the balance of payments. The ADB forecast that, despite the impact of the COVID-19 pandemic, Pakistan's economy was expected to grow by 2.6% in 2020 and 3.2% in 2021.

The positive assessment by the ADB was based on:

- The use of interest rates to counter inflationary pressures. The interest rate was reduced from 12.25% to 11% to offset the effects of COVID-19.
- A forecast inflation rate of 11.5% in 2020, falling to 8.3% in 2021.
- A reduction in the current account deficit to 2.8% GDP. This was achieved through the depreciation of the rupee and import restrictions. Import substitution and export promotion must continue.
- An increase in revenue from sales taxes on petrol, gas and electricity charges and an increase in the number of residents filing tax returns.
- High interest rates that continue to attract 'hot money' from corporate and private investors.

7   Explain how a Laffer curve can be used to analyse the effectiveness of fiscal policy in Pakistan.
8   Analyse how Pakistan's interest rate policy has managed to control inflation.
9   Analyse how the depreciation of Pakistan's rupee has affected other macroeconomic objectives.
10 Analyse how Pakistan's international trade policy has affected other macroeconomic objectives.

> **TIP**
>
> When considering the different macroeconomic objectives, remember that no single policy can ever hope to meet all objectives. Governments invariably use a combination of policies to meet their objectives.

47 Effectiveness of policy options to meet all macroeconomic objectives

Evaluation

11 Comment on the ADB's view that 'structural reforms of agriculture, industry and services are required to improve Pakistan's productivity and export competitiveness'.

PRACTICE QUESTIONS

Data response question

1 Discuss the benefits and costs of a high interest rate policy for Pakistan's economy.

Essay questions

1 Evaluate the effectiveness of supply-side policies in achieving the macroeconomic objectives of an economy.
2 Assess the view that fiscal policies alone cannot meet the macroeconomic objectives of low inflation and low unemployment.

Improve this answer

This is a sample answer to essay Q1.

> Supply-side policies are varied but all have the same objective, that of increasing aggregate supply. The nature of the policies is that they require a government to take a bigger role in the management of the economy **[K]**.
>
> A very relevant and widely used supply-side policy is for a government to increase its spending on education and training. If successful, this policy can have an important effect on all macroeconomic policy objectives. The purpose behind funding education and training is to provide a better, more qualified workforce. It can be seen as a form of investment that can enhance a country's future rate of increase in economic growth **[A]**. Increased spending on education and training is also likely to reduce unemployment. A new group of workers will be equipped with new skills that the labour market requires. If these workers had become unemployed for structural reasons, their re-training will have made them much more employable. Youth unemployment is a problem in many Asian countries. School leavers should be provided with the vocational skills they need to get a job, again reducing unemployment **[A]**.
>
> Spending on education and training over time can improve the productivity of a country. As the economy becomes more efficient, productivity will increase and the price of many goods and services could fall. Therefore, supply-side policies have contributed to controlling inflation. As the price of exports becomes more competitive, this may have a beneficial effect on the current account of the balance of payments through increased export sales **[A]**. A surplus on the balance of trade could lead to an appreciation of a country's foreign exchange rate.
>
> A final macroeconomic objective that can be influenced by supply-side policies is how to make the distribution of income more equitable. Education and training, especially where provided free of charge, can improve the incomes and future prospects of those from low-income backgrounds. A better trained and better educated person should always expect to receive higher pay than someone who is unskilled and who has had little education **[A]**.
>
> This example of supply-side policies is highly effective, since increased spending on education and training can affect all of the macroeconomic policy objectives of a country. It is also worth stressing that in all cases, the impact of education and training is positive **[E]**.

Your challenge

See whether you can improve this answer. The answer provides an evaluation of how increased spending on education and training can have a positive effect on each of the macroeconomic objectives. This is fine, but the wording of the question means that it is necessary to consider other types of supply-side policy as well as education and training. A diagram will enhance the quality of the answer. A better answer is given in the workbook answers – but write yours out first.

> Unit 11

International economic issues (A Level)

Chapter 48
Policies to correct disequilibrium in the balance of payments

LEARNING INTENTIONS

In this chapter you will:

- explain the components of the balance of payments: current account, financial account and capital account
- evaluate the effects of fiscal, monetary, supply-side, protectionist and exchange rate policies on the balance of payments
- explain the difference between expenditure-switching and expenditure-reducing policies.

KEY TERMS

Expenditure-reducing policy   Expenditure-switching policy   Net errors and omissions

Key skills exercises

Knowledge and understanding

To answer the questions in this chapter, you need to know and understand:

- the components of the balance of payments: current account, financial account, capital account
- the effect of fiscal, monetary, supply-side, protectionist and exchange rate policies on the balance of payments
- the difference between expenditure-switching and expenditure-reducing policies.

1 Describe what is meant by net errors and omissions in the balance of payments.

WORKED EXAMPLE FOR Q1

The purpose of this item is to ensure that the balance of payments always balances. It is required because of inaccuracies in collecting the mass of data that is needed **[K]**.

2 Explain what is included in the financial account of the balance of payments.

3 Explain what is included in the capital amount of the balance of payments.

4 Explain the difference between expenditure-switching and expenditure-reducing policies.

> **TIP**
>
> When looking at the balance of payments, it is useful to remember that the financial account is very important for many countries since, if in surplus, it can be used to offset a deficit in the current account. This is not always a good idea since it involves selling assets to pay for foreign goods and services.

48 Policies to correct disequilibrium in the balance of payments

Analysis

Indonesia's unusual balance of payments

Indonesia is a lower middle-income country that has experienced substantial growth over the past ten years. The growth has been mainly due to its exports of crude petroleum and natural gas. Indonesia is also one of the world's main exporters of rubber, along with agricultural products such as coffee, palm oil and spices.

An unusual feature of Indonesia's balance of payments is that it has had a substantial overall surplus, but a balance of trade deficit since 2018 (see Figure 48.1). In the early months of 2020, the deficit became a surplus.

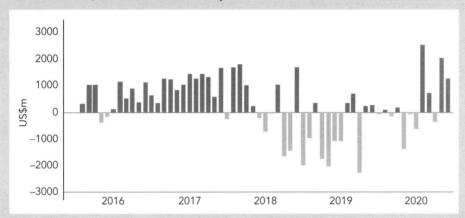

Figure 48.1: Indonesia's balance of trade, 2016–2020

Source: Trading Economics/Statistics Indonesia

The current account deficit is affected by the oil and gas trade deficit and the non-oil and gas trade surplus. The government has used import controls to reduce oil imports.

The surplus in the capital account and in financial transactions has continued to increase. This is seen as evidence that investors see a promising outlook for Indonesia's domestic economy in a global economy where future prospects are far from certain.

5 Give **two** examples of items that might be included in Indonesia's financial account of the balance of payments.

6 Give **two** examples of items that might be included in Indonesia's capital account of the balance of payments.

7 Analyse the effect of fiscal policies on the balance of payments.

8 Analyse the effect of monetary policies on the balance of payments.

9 Analyse the effect of supply-side policies on the balance of payments.

10 Analyse the effect of protectionist policies on the balance of payments.

11 Analyse the effect of exchange rate policies on the balance of payments.

12 Explain why Indonesia has disequilibrium in its balance of payments.

Evaluation

13 Comment on whether import controls are the best way to reduce Indonesia's current account deficit on the balance of trade.

PRACTICE QUESTIONS

Data response question

1. Explain why Indonesia has a current account surplus in the early part of 2020.

Essay questions

1. Evaluate the extent to which exchange rate policies are the best to use when a country has disequilibrium in the current account of the balance of payments.
2. Assess whether expenditure-switching or expenditure-reducing policies are best for a middle-income country to use to reduce a deficit in the current account of the balance of payments.

Improve this answer

This is a sample answer to essay Q2.

> Many middle-income countries face a deficit on the current account of the balance of payments. This deficit arises since the value of imports of goods and services exceeds the value of these exports. The problem is particularly serious where the deficit is persistent over a number of years. This usually indicates a structural imbalance in the economy. It is difficult to implement change when a country is heavily reliant on exports of agricultural products and low-end manufactured goods **[K]**.
>
> An expenditure-switching policy, as its name indicates, is designed to encourage consumers and firms to switch from buying foreign-produced products to buying domestically-produced products. Expenditure-switching policies include controls on imports such as tariffs and quotas, depreciation of the foreign exchange rate and supply-side policies to improve competitiveness **[A]**.
>
> A deliberate or planned depreciation of the exchange rate will increase the price of imported products relative to those that are domestically-produced. If the latter are good substitutes for imports and if the depreciation is strong enough, consumers can be expected to switch from foreign to home-produced goods. The extent of the switch will depend on the price elasticity of demand for imports – the more elastic it is, then the more successful the impact of the depreciation. The fall in the exchange rate is also designed to make a country's export prices more attractive than those of trading rivals. Again, depending on the price elasticity of demand, there should be an increase in value of exports, with a time lag **[A]**.
>
> An expenditure-reducing policy is different. This refers to any action taken by the government to reduce aggregate demand or total spending in an economy. Fiscal policy in the form of cuts in government spending or an increase in taxation can achieve the required contraction in aggregate demand **[A]**. It is at a cost. The level of employment can be expected to fall as a consequence of the reduction in aggregate demand. The domestic market for certain goods and services will contract. An interesting knock-on effect is that domestic firms may have an opportunity to increase their export sales due to the contraction in the domestic market **[E]**.
>
> In the case of a middle-income country, the cost of increased unemployment due to a cut in aggregate demand should not be under-estimated. It is also relevant to make clear that there is little scope for increasing taxation, except possibly in the case of an increase in a general sales tax (GST). These factors have to be considered when a country decides which is the best policy for it to use. It is most likely that this policy will be an expenditure-switching policy **[E]**.

48 Policies to correct disequilibrium in the balance of payments

CONTINUED

Your challenge

See whether you can improve this answer. This is a successful answer. The difference between an expenditure-switching and expenditure-reducing policy is made clear, with examples. The answer focuses on a middle-income country – this aspect of the question could be easily overlooked. The latter part of the answer includes relevant evaluation. The answer could be improved by real-world examples from a country the learner has studied. Your challenge is to write a new, second paragraph containing real-world examples. A better answer is given in the workbook answers – but write yours out first.

Chapter 49
Exchange rates

LEARNING INTENTIONS

In this chapter you will:

- identify the three main ways exchange rates are measured: nominal, real and trade-weighted exchange rates
- explain the difference between nominal and real exchange rates
- explain trade-weighted exchange rates
- analyse how exchange rates are determined under fixed and managed systems
- explain the difference between revaluation and devaluation of a fixed exchange rate
- analyse the causes of changes in the exchange rate under different exchange rate systems
- evaluate the effects of changing exchange rates on the external economy using the Marshall–Lerner condition and J-curve analysis.

KEY TERMS

Devaluation   Fixed exchange rate   J-curve effect   Managed system   Marshall-Lerner condition
Real exchange rate   Revaluation   Trade-weighted exchange rate

Key skills exercises

To answer the questions in this chapter, you need to know and understand:

- the difference between a nominal foreign exchange rate and a real exchange rate
- what is meant by a trade weighted exchanged rate
- the meaning of a fixed exchange rate
- the difference between devaluation and revaluation of a fixed exchange rate
- the meaning of a managed system
- the causes of changes in the exchange rate under different exchange rate systems
- the effects of changing exchange rates on the external economy
- the Marshall–Lerner condition
- the J-curve effect.

TIP

A common error made by learners is to be unclear on the difference between devaluation/revaluation and depreciation/appreciation of an exchange rate. Devaluation/revaluation refers to fixed exchange rates while depreciation/appreciation applies to managed float and freely floating exchange rate systems.

1 Explain how a real exchange rate differs from a nominal exchange rate.
2 Describe the meaning of a trade weighted exchange rate.
3 Describe the meaning of a fixed exchange rate.
4 Explain the difference between devaluation and revaluation of a fixed exchange rate.
5 Explain the meaning of a managed float.
6 Explain the Marshall–Lerner condition.
7 Explain the J-curve effect.

49 Exchange rates

> **WORKED EXAMPLE FOR Q7**
>
> The purpose of devaluing or depreciating an exchange rate is to improve a recurring deficit in the current account of the balance of payments. The J-curve indicates that this may not occur immediately following the devaluation or depreciation. It takes time for markets to adjust. The trade balance will improve provided the Marshall–Lerner condition holds. A trade surplus will then grow in time [A].

Analysis

Japan's decade of fluctuating exchange rates

The so-called Japanese model of industrialisation and high economic growth worked well for the Japanese economy in the 1980s. A high savings rate among the population reduced the cost of capital and promoted investment. These underpinned high rates of economic growth.

In more recent years, Japan's economic performance has puzzled economists. A series of fiscal stimuli, low interest rates and even 'helicopter money' has failed to lift Japan's economy. Economic growth has been negligible.

Notwithstanding, Japan has continued to record a surplus on the current account of the balance of payments. The value of exports has consistently been greater than the value of imports, although the gap is narrowing. A positive balance on the financial account has turned this into an even greater surplus.

Japan's currency, the yen, has experienced substantial change compared to the US dollar. This is shown below in Figure 49.1.

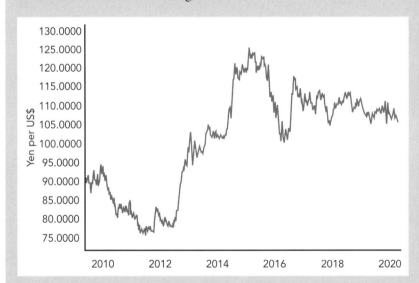

Figure 49.1: Yen-US dollar exchange rate, 2010–2020

Source: Macrotrends

8   Using the data in Figure 49.1, state whether the Japanese yen appreciated or depreciated against the US dollar over the period 2010 to 2020. Justify your answer.

9   Analyse the likely causes of changes in Japan's exchange rate against the US dollar for the period covered in Figure 49.1.

Evaluation

10 Evaluate the likely effects of a changing exchange rate on the external economy of Japan.

PRACTICE QUESTIONS

Multiple-choice question

1 Figure 49.1 shows the dollar–yen exchange rate over the period 2010–2020.

Which of these is the best explanation of the strength and direction of Japan's foreign exchange rate over the period?

	Strength of change	Change
A	depreciation	16.6%
B	depreciation	14.3%
C	appreciation	16.6%
D	appreciation	14.3%

Essay questions

1 Evaluate the extent to which the Marshall–Lerner condition and J-curve analysis are still reliable ways of monitoring the effects of changing exchange rates on the external economy.

2 Assess the benefits and costs of a fixed exchange rate system and of a managed system.

Improve this answer

This is a sample answer to essay Q2.

> A fixed exchange rate system is one where the exchange rate is set by the government. An example is where a country's exchange is fixed relative to the US dollar, the main currency used for international transactions. Most of the countries still using a fixed exchange rate are in the Middle East and include Bahrain, Jordan, Oman and Saudi Arabia. A currency is also technically fixed when its exchange rate is pegged to another currency – this seeks to keep the value of the currency stable. Most of the Caribbean Islands, for example, peg their currencies to the US dollar, since most of their trade transactions, especially for tourism, are carried out in dollars **[K]**.
>
> A fixed exchange rate has certain advantages. The biggest benefit is that in international trade, the price of exports and imports can be established at the time trading contracts are being drawn up. This certainty is particularly important for small economies. It is particularly beneficial where a country has an extensive international tourist industry where contracts with hotels and airlines are often drawn up a year or so before the holidays take place **[A]**.
>
> A disadvantage of fixed exchange rates is that it is invariably necessary for the central bank to maintain the exchange rate through the buying and selling of foreign currency reserves. If the supply of a currency on the exchange market is increasing due to, say, US consumers buying more imports from a country, the central bank will buy enough of its currency to keep the rate of exchange fixed. The government also increases interest rates in order to attract hot money flows.
>
> A second disadvantage of a fixed rate system is that the government risks sacrificing other macroeconomic objectives in order to maintain its fixed rate exchange. A typical example is where a government raises interest rates to protect its currency. High interest rates may reduce aggregate demand and increase unemployment. This is the price the government has to pay for keeping a fixed exchange rate. Using reserves and increasing interest rates may not be a longer-term solution – the inevitable outcome could be that devaluation is the only remaining policy option **[A]**.

CONTINUED

Major currencies such as the US dollar, the euro, the Yen and the Chinese RMB have managed systems against other currencies. The exchange rate is based on the supply and demand for a currency, in other words, it is determined by market forces. A change in the exchange rate becomes indicative of the strength or weakness of a currency in the global market. Under a managed system, a currency depreciates and appreciates on a regular daily basis **[A]**.

A currency depreciates when there is a decrease in demand or an increase in supply for a currency. The outcome of a depreciation is that the price of exports becomes slightly more competitive while the price of imported goods increases. It is hoped that the depreciation will increase the demand for imports by other countries which, if it occurs, could over time see the currency appreciating.

There are advantages of a managed system. An obvious one is that reserves of foreign exchange do not have to be regularly moved to meet problems of imbalance on the current account of the balance of payments. It is also easier with a managed system for an economy to restore balance in the current account of its balance of payments **[A]**.

The main disadvantage of a managed system is that in trading with other countries, it is difficult to estimate what the exchange rate might be in a few weeks' time, let alone in a few months' time when goods may be delivered. A second disadvantage is that if a currency depreciates in value, the price of imported goods will increase. This may cause domestic firms to be not too bothered about keeping their own prices competitive.

It is clear that fixed exchange rate and managed systems have advantages and disadvantages. It is not possible to say which is the best, since the system that a country adopts will normally be a function of the type of economy. The major currencies are best as managed systems. A fixed exchange rate system, though, is more preferable for smaller economies, especially those that have a fundamental trading relationship with, say, the USA and therefore fix their currency to the US dollar **[E]**.

Your challenge

See whether you can improve this answer. This is a successful answer to the question. It covers the advantages and disadvantages of each type of exchange rate system, and concludes with a paragraph of evaluation. Your challenge is to add a new second paragraph of explanation that includes a diagram. A better answer is given in the workbook answers – but write yours out first.

Chapter 50
Economic development

LEARNING INTENTIONS

In this chapter you will:

- describe how economies are classified in terms of their development and level of national income
- evaluate indicators of living standards and economic development including real per capita national income statistics, purchasing power parity, non-monetary indicators and composite indicators
- explain the Kuznets curve
- compare economic growth rates and living standards over time and between countries.

KEY TERMS

Development traps   Human Development Index (HDI)   Kuznets curve   Measurable Economic Welfare (MEW)
Multidimensional Poverty Index (MPI)   Poverty cycles   Purchasing Power Parity (PPP)   Shadow economy

Key skills exercises

Knowledge and understanding

To answer the questions in this chapter, you need to know and understand:

- how an economy is classified according to income
- the meaning of a poverty cycle
- the components of the Human Development Index (HDI)
- the nature of Measurable Economic Welfare (MEW)
- the indicators used for the Multidimensional Poverty Index (MPI)
- the significance of the shadow economy
- the Kuznets curve
- the meaning of Purchasing Power Parity (PPP).

1 Explain the meaning of the poverty cycle.
2 Explain the components of the Human Development Index (HDI).
3 Explain the meaning of Measurable Economic Welfare (MEW).
4 Explain the measures used for the Multidimensional Poverty Index (MPI).
5 Describe what is meant by the shadow economy.
6 Explain the Kuznets curve.

TIP

Composite indices of economic development like the Human Development Index are shown as a value between 0 and 1, to three decimal places. This can be taken to mean that all data that is used is accurate to this level of detail. This is not so, especially in countries that have weak data collection systems. The HDI measure is most widely used and understood. Use some examples where possible.

Analysis

Bhutan's Gross National Happiness (GNH) Index

In 1972, the Fourth King of Bhutan stated that 'Gross National Happiness is more important than Gross Domestic Product.' Since 1972, Bhutan's economic progress has been firmly rooted in promoting sustainable development, with equal importance being given to non-economic aspects of well-being, as well as to economic measures such as living standards. Non-economic measures include health, education, cultural diversity and resilience, and ecological diversity and resilience.

Table 50.1 shows the rank and value of the GNH Index for selected countries drawn from Bhutan's 2020 Gross National Happiness Index.

Country	Rank	Index	Country	Rank	Index
Finland	1	7.809	Indonesia	84	5.286
UK	13	7.165	China	92	5.120
USA	18	6.940	Bhutan	95	5.082
Mauritius	49	6.101	South Africa	109	4.814
Pakistan	66	5.653	Sri Lanka	130	4.327
Malaysia	82	5.384	India	144	3.693

Table 50.1: Gross National Happiness Index, selected countries

The GNH Index is used to support government policy-making in Bhutan. The potential effects on the Index are measured before any policies are implemented. The overall objective is to maximise the GNH.

7   Analyse why some countries have a high HDI ranking and why others have a low HDI ranking.

8   Explain how the index of Measurable Economic Welfare (MEW) provides a fuller picture of living standards than just GDP per head.

Evaluation

9   Comment on how Bhutan's approach to policy making could be applied by other countries.

PRACTICE QUESTIONS

Multiple-choice question

1   A basket of goods and services sells for $2000 in the USA, but the same basket sells for £1000 in the UK. In terms of purchasing power parity, which of these statements is true?

   A   The dollar-pound exchange rate is $2 equals £1.
   B   The dollar-pound exchange rate is $1 equals £2.
   C   The basket of goods and services is twice the price in the USA compared to the UK.
   D   The basket of goods and services is half the price in the USA compared to the UK.

CONTINUED

WORKED EXAMPLE FOR Q1

A.

Purchasing power parity means that a unit of a currency can buy the same basket of goods and services in all countries. So something that sells for $2 in the USA will sell for £1 in the UK on a purchasing power parity basis. C and D are not correct as they are not in terms of purchasing power parity.

Essay questions

1 Evaluate which is the best way of measuring differences in the level of development in middle-income countries.
2 Assess the strengths and weaknesses of the Human Development Index (HDI) as a means of establishing policy priorities for economic development.

Improve this answer

This is a sample answer to essay Q2.

> Economic development is a broad concept. Historically, economists saw economic development largely in terms of variations in GDP per head. Countries with a low GDP per head were seen as being less developed than countries with a higher GDP per head.
>
> The UN's Human Development Index is an established composite measure of economic development. GDP per head is one of its variables. Other variables relate to education and how long people can expect to live. The HDI is an average of these measures and is published for over 150 countries. The latest report shows that South Asia is making the most progress in terms of human development. As might be expected, developed Western economies like Norway and Finland are at the top of the rankings, with the least developed sub-Saharan African economies at the bottom of the list **[K]**.
>
> The purpose of the HDI is from a policy standpoint. Its purpose is to get those responsible for making policy decisions to see how what is proposed affects that country's level of human development. A key issue for them to consider is why two countries with the same level of GDP per head have widely differing values for their HDI. Where this is the case, the government needs to assess whether it is putting its resources into projects and policies that provide a wider benefit for its population.
>
> The HDI is a useful and regularly available indicator of human development. Although it covers variables other than GDP per head, it does not include data on some of the wider development issues such as income distribution, unemployment and gender inequality. **[K]**

Your challenge

See whether you can improve this answer. This is a weak answer. There are some valid points, but these tend to be made in a superficial way. The description of the HDI is poor. More should be included on the use of the HDI measure. References to 'strengths' and 'weaknesses' as directed by the question would enhance the answer's structure. A better answer is given in the workbook answers – but write yours out first.

Chapter 51
Characteristics of countries at different levels of development

LEARNING INTENTIONS

In this chapter you will:

- explain how birth rate, death rate, infant mortality rate and net migration are measured
- analyse the causes of changes in birth rate, death rate, infant mortality and net migration
- explain the concept of the optimum population
- explain how the level of urbanisation changes as countries develop
- explain how income distribution can be measured
- calculate and interpret the Gini coefficient
- analyse and draw Lorenz curves
- explain employment composition in terms of primary, secondary and tertiary sectors
- analyse the pattern of trade at different levels of development.

KEY TERMS

Birth rate   Death rate   Demographers   Dependency ratio   Infant mortality rate   Lorenz curve
Natural increase in population   Net migration   Net migration rate   Optimum population
Positive net migration   Primary sector   Secondary sector   Tertiary sector

Key skills exercises

To answer the questions in this chapter, you need to know and understand:

- how to measure birth rate, death rate, infant mortality rate and net migration
- what determines changes in birth rate, death rate, infant mortality rate and net migration
- the meaning of optimum population
- how the level of urbanisation changes as countries develop
- how to measure income distribution
- how to calculate the Gini coefficient and know what it means
- what is shown by a Lorenz curve
- the employment composition of an economy
- the pattern of trade at different levels of development.

1 Define birth rate.
2 Define death rate.
3 Define infant mortality rate.

> **TIP**
>
> Make a list of key economic data for a country or countries you have studied. You can use this information to add relevance to your arguments.

4   Explain what is meant by net migration.

5   Explain the meaning of optimum population.

6   Describe how to measure income distribution.

7   Explain what is shown by a Lorenz curve.

8   Describe the employment composition of an economy.

Analysis

When will Thailand reach the Lewis Turning Point?

Thailand's economy has experienced substantial change in moving from a low-income country to an upper middle-income country. Even so, in 2020 31% of the working population were employed in agriculture; 23% were in manufacturing and 46% in services.

Like other emerging economies in Southeast Asia, Thailand is facing problems of a declining and aging population. Figure 51.1 shows the expected change in the age distribution of the population in 2050 compared with the age distribution in 2020.

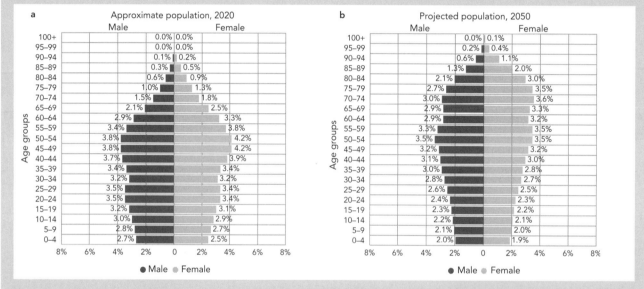

Figure 51.1: Population pyramids, Thailand 2020 and 2050 (projected)

Source: UN WPP

Thailand's economy will continue to depend on the on-going shift of workers from agriculture to other parts of the economy. There will come a point, probably between 2030 and 2040, where surplus rural labour becomes fully absorbed elsewhere in the economy. Known as the Lewis Turning Point, it will mean that from this point, wages in manufacturing especially will have to rise. This is good news for all workers employed in manufacturing. From this point, Thailand may have to accept more migrant workers from elsewhere in Asia.

9   Analyse how the level of urbanisation changes as countries develop.

51 Characteristics of countries at different levels of development

WORKED EXAMPLE FOR Q9

Most high-income countries have a high percentage of their population living in urban areas. Typical examples are Japan, the USA and UK. It should also be remembered that many low- and middle-income countries have high concentrations of an urban population. Examples include Mumbai, Shanghai, Lagos and Kinshasa **[K]**.

A contributory factor has been the way in which there has been a regular cycle of drift from rural areas to large cities. So, as economies develop, it is quite usual for there to be an increasing proportion of the population living in urban areas **[A]**.

10 Analyse how the pattern of trade varies at different levels of development.

11 Analyse the main projected changes to Thailand's projected population between 2020 and 2050.

12 Analyse why wages in manufacturing in Thailand are expected to increase after the Lewis Turning point.

Evaluation

13 Comment upon how Thailand's economy will have to adapt to meet the needs of an aging population.

PRACTICE QUESTIONS

Multiple-choice question

1 The figure below shows a Lorenz curve.
   Suppose there is a shift in the area of inequality from A to B. Explain what this shift shows.

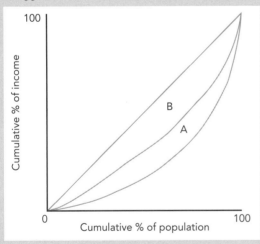

   A The distribution of income is now more equal.
   B The distribution of wealth and the distribution of income and now more equal.
   C The distribution of income is now less equal.
   D The distribution of wealth and the distribution of income and now less equal.

CONTINUED

Essay questions

1 Evaluate how economists compare the characteristics of high-income countries with those of middle-income and low-income countries.
2 Assess how the employment composition and pattern of trade of economies changes at different levels of development.

Improve this answer

This is a sample answer to essay Q1.

> The World Bank defines a high-income country as one that has a GNI per head of over $12 375. A low-income country is one where GNI per head is less than $1026. Middle-income economies lie between these two extremes, with an upper middle-income economy having a GNI per head about $3995, but below the bottom figure for a high-income country [K]. An obvious starting point for any comparison is to recognise the differences in these terms. This is because the level of GNI per head clearly affects the many other characteristics between the different types of country.
>
> There are many statistics that can be used to make comparisons between high-income countries and others. A relevant starting point is to consider some demographic measures such as birth rates, death rates, life expectancy and infant mortality rates. In general, high-income countries have lower birth rates and death rates, higher life expectancy and lower infant mortality rates compared to other types of economies. A further related characteristic is the dependency ratio, a measure of the proportion of economically inactive people compared to the total labour force. For cultural as well as economic reasons, the dependency ratio is considerably lower in high-income countries compared to other countries [A].
>
> A second set of characteristics that can be used are statistics of employment for different sectors of the economy. In most high-income countries, for example, the percentage of the workforce employed in agriculture will be very small, often just 2 or 3% of the working population. In low-income countries, this figure is more likely to be over 50 or 60% of the working population. The percentage of employment in manufacturing is also variable, although it is difficult to generalise. This is because all economies have some manufacturing sector, typically accounting for 15–20% of the employed population. In the most developed economies, and also in China and India, employment in the service sector is now dominant. This is particularly the case in the growing IT and knowledge-based services sector [A].
>
> A third set of statistics that can be used to make comparisons are data on the composition of a country's trade. Middle-income economies are now the driving force of exports of manufactured goods, such as vehicles, electronics and garments. Production has continued to divert from high-income countries. Cheaper manufactured goods tend to be produced in lower-middle-income countries. It is also usually the case that, unlike high-income countries, most other economies do not have the diversified product range that makes up their exports [A].

Your challenge

See whether you can improve this answer. It has the potential to be a high-quality answer. The factual base is sound, but at times more explicit data, rather than generalisations, would enhance the answer. The first paragraph could be shortened to allow more time to spend on answering the question. Some real-world data or examples should be added, for example demographic data, data on employment structure and the composition of trade. You could use data from a country you have studied. The answer lacks evaluation – this could be a paragraph that assesses the characteristics that have been used. A better answer is given in the workbook answers – but write yours out first.

Chapter 52
Relationship between countries at different levels of development

LEARNING INTENTIONS

In this chapter you will:

- describe different forms of international aid
- explain reasons for giving aid
- evaluate the effects and importance of aid
- analyse the role of trade and investment between countries
- define the meaning of multinational companies
- evaluate the activities and consequences of multinational companies
- define the meaning of foreign direct investment
- evaluate the consequences of foreign direct investment
- explain the causes of external debt
- evaluate the consequences of external debt
- explain the role of the International Monetary Fund
- explain the role of the World Bank.

KEY TERMS

Aid   Bilateral aid   Emerging economies   Foreign direct investment (FDI)   Multilateral aid
Tied aid   Untied aid   Virtuous cycle

Key skills exercises

Knowledge and understanding

To answer the questions in this chapter, you need to know and understand:

- the types of international aid
- the reasons for giving aid
- the effects and importance of aid
- the role of trade and investment between countries
- the meaning of a multinational company
- the activities and consequences of multinational companies
- the meaning of foreign direct investment

TIP

Learners sometimes confuse the roles of the International Monetary Fund and the World Bank. You should be clear as to how their work differs. Broad details are usually all that is needed.

- the consequences of foreign direct investment
- the causes and consequences of external debt
- the role of the International Monetary Fund
- the role of the World Bank.

1 Describe the main types of international aid.
2 Explain the reasons for giving international aid.
3 Describe the meaning of a multinational company.
4 Explain the activities of multinational companies.
5 Describe the meaning of foreign direct investment.
6 Explain the causes of external debt for an economy.

WORKED EXAMPLE FOR Q6

The main cause of external debt is structural weakness on the current account of the balance of payments. Many low- and lower middle-income economies are in this position due to their heavy dependence on the export of agricultural produce. These countries invariably rely on costly imports of fuel, manufactured goods and consumer goods. Imports are more than exports. Countries have to borrow to fund recurring deficits. Further reasons are if the currency depreciates, or there is an unforeseen collapse in the export market following the financial crash or the COVID-19 pandemic [A].

7 Describe the role of the IMF.
8 Describe the role of the World Bank.

Analysis

Multinational companies in India

Compared to other parts of Asia, India was relatively slow to open its economy to multinational companies (MNCs). This is no longer the case – India's growing economy has attracted many new MNCs in a diverse range of business. Examples include:

- IT services – Microsoft Corporation, IBM
- Electronics – Sony Corporation, LG, Samsung
- Vehicles – Toyota, Mercedes-Benz, VW Group
- Food and drink – Coca Cola, KFC, Nestlé.

One reason for the Indian government's lack of enthusiasm for MNCs has been the desire to protect its own conglomerates, such as Tata Group and Reliance Industries. With a growing population, especially of young graduates, it is important that all major companies continue to provide jobs and investment for India's sustained economic progress.

MNCs promote the flow of Foreign Direct Investment (FDI) into India, creating a valuable capital inflow into the balance of payments. Another benefit is technology transfer. When an MNC like Toyota sets up a new car assembly plant in India, the Japanese company imports new machinery, technology and expertise, all of which are designed to increase productivity. A third benefit is that once established, MNCs can export their products. The Japanese company Suzuki, for example, has joined up with Maruti, the Indian car manufacturer, to export Indian-made vehicles to other countries in South Asia.

9 Analyse the role of trade and investment between India and other countries.
10 Analyse the likely consequences for the Indian economy of an increase in FDI by multinational companies.

Evaluation

11 Discuss whether the benefits of multinational companies to the Indian economy outweigh the likely costs.

PRACTICE QUESTIONS

Multiple-choice question

1 A Chinese multinational company finances investment for a new pharmaceutical factory in Pakistan.
   Which of these explains the effect of this investment on Pakistan's balance of payments?
   A a credit in the balance of trade
   B a credit in the capital account
   C a credit in the financial account
   D a credit in the trade in services

Essay questions

1 'Trade not aid' is a long-established view as to how growth should be achieved in low- and some middle-income countries.
   Assess the extent to which this view is still applicable.
2 Evaluate the consequences of increasing external debt for low-income and lower middle-income countries.

Improve this answer

This is a sample answer to essay Q1.

> 'Trade not aid' is a strategy that has been strongly advocated to enhance the economic development of low and some middle-income countries for many years. The purpose of promoting trade as a policy is that the onus rests firmly with the country concerned. This is in contrast to aid policies which tend in most cases to be determined by the donor [K].
>
> It is clear from the most recent rounds of talks at the WTO that high-income countries are in control of negotiations. A sore point for many low- and lower middle-income countries is the subsidies that continue to be paid to agricultural producers in high-income countries, notably the USA and EU [K]. To make matters worse, the USA and the EU impose high tariffs on many agricultural products from poorer countries that do not have special arrangements with them. What poorer countries want is fair trade, or trade on terms that are fair to all [A].
>
> Low- and some middle-income countries have a range of agricultural products and low cost manufactured goods such as trainers and sports clothing that are demanded by consumers in high-income countries. Through trade, revenue from such exports enters the circular flow of income. It is a credit item in the current account of the balance of payments as well as triggering a multiplier effect in terms of total spending and employment. On the down side, the terms of trade for most poorer countries have deteriorated, meaning that more needs to be exported for the same amount of imported goods [A].

CONTINUED

Some middle-income countries benefit from investments by multinational companies such as Nestlé, Procter and Gamble, Samsung etc. Once established, these MNCs will produce goods not only for the domestic market but also for export. These exports are an important credit item in the current account. MNCs generate employment and can provide the foundation for what is called 'export-led growth' **[A]**.

Trade can therefore be the basis for growth in low-income and more particularly, lower middle-income countries. The global trade environment is not as free as it ought to be. With the USA at the forefront, there are increased restrictions on trade, meaning that the best use is not being made of the world's scarce resources. This state of affairs does little to help the well-being of poorer countries and to realise the economic growth and development they need **[E]**.

Your challenge

See whether you can improve this answer. The answer contains some relevant analysis of trade issues. It is applied and relevant to the question. The last paragraph has some valid evaluation. The weakness of the answer is that the aid aspect of the question is largely ignored. A better approach is to consider aid policies alongside trade policies and to come to a conclusion whether the view that 'trade not aid' remains applicable. A better answer is given in the workbook answers – but write yours out first.

Chapter 53
Globalisation

LEARNING INTENTIONS

In this chapter you will:
- define the meaning of globalisation
- analyse the causes and consequences of globalisation
- analyse the difference between a free trade area, a customs union, a monetary union and full economic union
- explain the difference between trade creation and trade diversion.

KEY TERMS

Customs union   Free trade area   Full economic union   Globalisation   Monetary union
Trade bloc   Trade creation   Trade diversion

Key skills exercises

Knowledge and understanding

To answer the questions in this chapter, you need to know and understand:
- the meaning of globalisation
- the causes and consequences of globalisation
- the characteristics of trade blocs: a free trade area, a customs union, monetary union and full economic union
- the difference between trade creation and trade diversion.

1. Define globalisation.
2. Explain the causes of globalisation.
3. Explain the characteristics of a free trade area, a customs union, a monetary union and a full economic union.
4. Explain the difference between trade creation and trade diversion.

WORKED EXAMPLE FOR Q4

These terms are used to describe how a country's trade can be expected to change when it becomes a member of a customs union. Trade creation is a situation where more expensive products are replaced by lower-priced products that are sourced from another member of the customs union. This is consistent with the principle of comparative advantage. Trade diversion is different. Trade diversion is where a member of the customs union buys imports from another member rather than from a more efficient producer outside the customs union. This situation is an inefficient allocation of resources. It is a common criticism of a static effect when a new member joins a customs union **[A]**.

TIP

When discussing or writing about the topics in this chapter, it is very helpful to use real examples of free trade areas and customs unions. Make sure that your examples are current ones, as this subject is one of almost continuous change.

Analysis

> **Deglobalisation: An Unfortunate Reality**
>
> Few would dispute the benefits of globalisation. Especially through the growth of trade, the countries of the world, with few exceptions, have become firmly interconnected. Globalisation has driven economic growth for much of the twenty-first century.
>
> Deglobalisation is now an unfortunate reality. In 2019, for the first time in many years, world trade fell sharply. What was the main reason? Increasing trade tensions, in particular between the USA and some of its trading partners. The dispute with China over tariffs and the value of the yuan was dragging on. The USA introduced tariffs on imports from Argentina and Brazil, partly to offset their currency devaluations. The USA also threatened 100% tariffs on imports of French champagne and new rates of tariff on cars manufactured in the EU. In Asia, India restricted exports of food and pharmaceuticals. This was seen as a deliberate act of protection. While all of this was happening, the UK was struggling to reach a Brexit deal to leave the European Union.
>
> In 2020, the global economy was hit unexpectedly by the COVID-19 pandemic. Its impact will be long-lasting, throwing the global economy into an era where further deglobalisation is inevitable. Trade relations will inevitably become even more protectionist. The World Trade Organization appears to be powerless to stop this happening. There are also fears that shipping and air freight charges will increase in real terms as part of a global strategy to cut back on carbon emissions. All in all, deglobalisation would seem to be an unfortunate reality.

5   Analyse the consequences of globalisation for low-income and lower middle-income countries.

Evaluation

6   Assess the view that trade wars and the COVID-19 pandemic have accelerated the demise of globalisation.

PRACTICE QUESTIONS

Multiple-choice question

1   A new member joins a customs union.
    Which of the following is an explanation of how trade diversion affects this new member?

	Price of product	Where product is sourced
A	cheaper	within the customs union
B	cheaper	outside the customs union
C	more expensive	within the customs union
D	more expensive	outside the customs union

53 Globalisation

CONTINUED

Essay questions

1 Evaluate the view that the benefits of globalisation are greater for high-income countries than for low- and middle-income countries.
2 Assess the view that free trade areas and free trade agreements provide far more benefits than can be obtained from a customs union.

Improve this answer

This is a sample answer to essay Q2.

> The World Trade Organization promotes a trading system based on free trade whereby all members are treated fairly. Economic theory strongly advocates multilateral free trade as providing the most efficient allocation of scarce resources. In principle and in reality, free trade reduces prices and the cost of living. Consumers are able to benefit from a greater choice of goods and services. Free trade raises incomes, increases employment and stimulates economic growth [K].
>
> A free trade agreement or free trade area consists of a group of countries that gradually agree to eliminate trade barriers between themselves. A recent example is the Comprehensive Agreement for Trans-Pacific Partnership signed by 11 countries and which aims to eliminate tariffs on all trade between themselves. An example is that farmers in Canada, Australia and New Zealand now have tariff-free access into the lucrative Japanese market, something that was previously denied. There are benefits for other members such as Vietnam and Malaysia. These countries are now able to export manufactured goods with few constraints to other members [K].
>
> There are numerous benefits of free trade agreements. Increased competition between members means that only the most efficient producers will survive. There is the added benefit of being able to take advantage of economies of scale, therefore lowering the average costs of production as the scale of the firm increases. This is another case of lower prices for consumers. The enlarged market will also prove to be attractive for MNCs that are looking to expand their activities to an enlarged market with no trade barriers [A].
>
> A customs union consists of a group of countries that agree to remove all trade barriers between themselves. In addition, and this is the main difference compared to a free trade area, members adopt a common trade policy towards non-members. Central to this policy is the erection of a CET, common external tariff. The CET is set at various levels and is highly protective of the trade interests of members of the customs union. Tariffs tend to be high on products that can be produced by customs union members. This is so in the EU which also has a common market and labour mobility within its structure. [A].
>
> A customs union by definition is protective of the interest of its members. This means that there are various forms of discrimination with trade with third-party countries. This limits the benefits of a customs union. In contrast, a free trade area has benefits in terms of specialisation but without the negatives associated with a CET. Trade policy with non-members is usually left for individual members to decide [E].

Your challenge

See whether you can improve this answer. This is a successful answer which contains sound analysis in context. The answer focuses on the benefits as directed by the wording of the question. An assessment of the costs of free trade areas and customs unions is not required. The last paragraph contains some limited evaluation. A better final paragraph is given in the workbook answers – but write yours out first.

Acknowledgements

The author and publishers acknowledge the following sources of copyright material and are grateful for the permissions granted. While every effort has been made, it has not always been possible to identify the sources of all the material used, or to trace all copyright holders. If any omissions are brought to our notice, we will be happy to include the appropriate acknowledgements on reprinting.

Figure 1.1 Data from Centre for Monitoring Indian Economy (CMIE). Used with the permission of CMIE; Chapter 2 Excerpt from 'What is economics? Understanding the discipline'. Used with the permission of American Economic Association; Figure 14.1 from 'Poverty and economic inequality from Vietnamese citizens' perspective in 2018. Used with the permission of Vietnam Law & Legal Forum; Figure 16.1 data from Statistics Mauritius. Used with the permission of Statistics Mauritius; Figure 19.1 Data from Centre for Monitoring Indian Economy (CMIE). Used with the permission of CMIE; Table 21.1 Data from Trading Economics; Figure 39.1 from Rawson Property Group blog article 2008. Used with the permission from Rawson Property Group; Figure 45.1 & Chapter 45 excerpt from SGI (Sustainable Governance Indicators) South Korea, Economic Policies. Used with the permission of Bertelsmann Stiftung; Figure 46.1 from 'The Phillips curve still holds', Copyright 2017 National Bank of Canada. All rights reserved. Reproduced with the permission. Data from BLS and Atlanta Fed; Figure 48.1 taken from Trading Economics

Cover image MirageC/Getty Images

From the author: I would like to thank Susan Ross of Ross Economics and Editorial Services Ltd for her fastidious work in ensuring what I have produced is appropriate for international students. My thanks are also to Rosalyn Scott, Biljana Savikj and Naomi Sklar at Cambridge University Press for their comments on the draft manuscript and for managing the production process. Thanks also to my daughter Emily for assistance with word processing.